DATE DUE

JY 13 '95			

DEMCO 38-297

GULF OF MEXICO

Brownsville
Matamoros
Monterrey
Saltillo
Ciudad Victoria
Tampico
MIAMI
CAPE SABLE
Key West
FLORIDA KEYS
Straits of Florida
Nassau
GRAND BAHAMA
GREAT ABACO
ELEUTHERA
CAT
SAN SALVADO
ANDROS
LONG
ACKLINS

Tropic of Cancer

HAVANA Guanabacoa
Marianao Matanzas
Pinar del Río Cárdenas
Cienfuegos Santa Clara
Sancti Spíritus
Trinidad Ciego de Avila
Nuevitas
Camagüey
Holguín
Manzanillo
Santiago de Cuba
Guantánamo
PUNTA MAISI
ILE DE LA
GONAVE
Windward Passage

San Luis Potosí
Ciudad Mante
Tuxpan
Papantla de Olarte
Nautla

Progreso
Sisal
Mérida
YUCATAN
Temax
Valladolid
C. CATOCHE
ISLA DE COZUMEL

Yucatan Channel
C. SAN ANTONIO
ISLA DE LA JUVENTUD
GRAND CAYMAN (Br.)
Montego Bay
Spanish Town
JAMAICA
Kingston
Denham
Port Antonio

MEXICO CITY
Puebla
Orizaba
Veracruz
Xalapa
Campeche
CAMPECHE
QUINTANA ROO
Ciudad Chetumal
(Payo Obispo)
Bahía de Chetumal
Belize City
TURNEFFE

Ciudad del Carmen
Laguna de Terminos
Bahía de Campeche

TABASCO
Villahermosa
Minatitlán
Coatzacoalcos
(Puerto México)
San Andrés Tuxtla

Oaxaca
OAXACA
Tehuantepec
Salina Cruz
Juchitán
CHIAPAS
San Cristóbal de las Casas
Tuxtla Gutiérrez
Comitán

Belmopan
BELIZE
Gulf of Honduras
ISLAS DE LA BAHIA
Pto. Cortés
La Ceiba
Tela
Trujillo

Golfo de Tehuantepec

Quezaltenango
Mazatenango
GUATEMALA
Tacaná
Totonicapán
Antigua
Guatemala
Pto. Barrios

HONDURAS
Juticalpa
Comayagua
Tegucigalpa

SANTA ANA
San Salvador
EL SALVADOR
San Miguel
Matagalpa

Golfo de Fonseca
NICARAGUA
León
Managua
Granada
Bluefields
Lago de Nicaragua

San Juan del Sur

CENTRAL AMERICA

COSTA RICA
San José Limón
Cartago
Puntarenas
Golfo de los Mosquitos
ISTMO
Colón
PANAMA
Portobello
Golfo del Darién
Lorica
Sincelejo
Magangué
Montería

PANAMA
Panamá
David
Santiago
Antón
PEN DE AZUERO
Golfo de Panamá

Golfo Dulce

Santa Marta
Barranquilla
Soledad
Cartagena

Barrancabermeja

Medellín
Sonson
Manizales
Pereira
Armenia
Ibagué
Girardot
Buenaventura
Cali
Palmira

ISLA DEL COCO
(Costa Rica)

ISLA DE MALPELO
(Colombia)

PACIFIC OCEAN

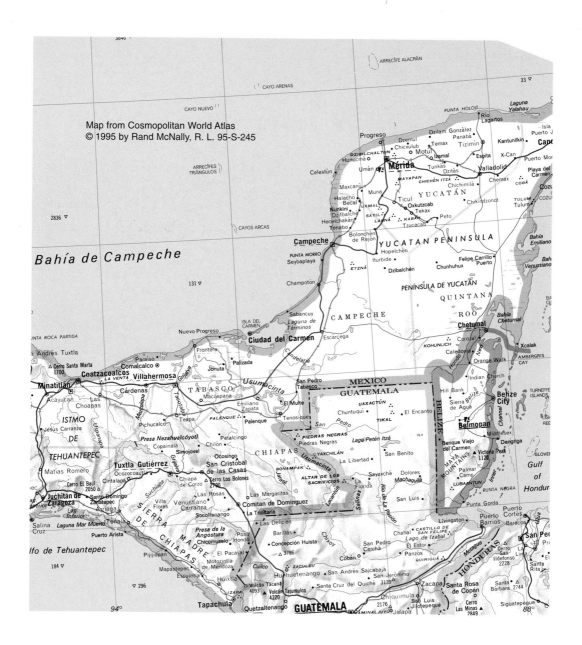

Map from Cosmopolitan World Atlas
© 1995 by Rand McNally, R. L. 95-S-245

Enchantment of the World

BELIZE

By Marion Morrison

Consultant for Belize: George I. Blanksten, Ph.D., Professor Emeritus of
Political Science, Northwestern University, Evanston, Illinois

CHILDREN'S PRESS®
A Division of Grolier Publishing
New York • London • Hong Kong • Sydney
Danbury, Connecticut

Two Mayan women selling necklaces to passing tourists

Project Editor and Design: Jean Blashfield Black
Photo Research: Feldman & Associates, Inc.

Library of Congress Cataloging-in-Publication Data

Morrison, Marion.
    Belize / by Marion Morrison. — (Enchantment of the world)
        p. cm. — (Enchantment of the world)
    Includes index.
    Summary: Describes the history, geography, economy,
government and customs of the Central American country
formerly known as British Honduras.
    ISBN 0-516-02639-9
    1. Belize—Juvenile literature. [1. Belize.] I. Title. II.
Series.
    F1443.2.M67 1996
    972.82—dc20   95-36158
                                                    CIP
                                                    AC

Picture Acknowledgments:

AP/Wide World Photos, Inc.: 32 (left and right); 54 (left).
The Bettman Archive: 35 (left and right).
D. D. Bryant Stock Photo: © Joe Cavanaugh, 23 (bottom left); © L.
B. Bastian, 39, 58 (center right); © Byron Augustin, 45, 67, 78, 86
(right); © D. Donne Bryant, 29, 51 (right); © Stewart Aitchison, 58

(top); © Peter Chartrand, 73 (top), 77 (right), 104; © Filmteam,
89 (left); © J. P Courau, 111; © John Curtis, 102 (right).
Dave G. Houser: © James C. Simmons, 12, 18, 105 (left), 106
(left), 109 (right); © Dave G. Houser, 90 (right).
H. Armstrong Roberts: © J. Irwin, 8-9; © Frink/Waterhouse,
14; © Suzanne Marger, 25 (bottom right); © D. Degnan, 86 (left).
Chip & Rosa Maria Peterson: © Chip & Rosa Maria Peterson, 96.
Photri: 22 (left); 73 (bottom left); © Mel M. Baughman, 84
(right); © James C. Simmons, 90 (left), 95.
Reuters/Bettman: 54 (right).
Root Resources: © Gail Nachel, 23 (top right); © Ben Goldstein,
23 (bottom right).
South American Pictures: © Chris Sharp, 5, 17 (left), 20 (top
left and bottom left), 42 (top and bottom), 57, 70, 73 (center
right), 73 (bottom right), 80 (left), 92 (top and bottom), 98, 101
(left and right), 109 (left); © Tony Morrison, Cover, 21, 33, 56, 74
(left), 76 (left and right), 77 (left), 83 (right), 87, 89 (right), 97
(right); © Charlotte Lipson, 63.
Tom Stack & Associates: © Wendy Shattil/Bob Rozinski, 10,
37; © Mary Clay, 20 (top right), 24 (left), 83 (left); © Byron
Augustin, 48, 80 (right); © Barbara Von Hoffman, 105 (right).
Stock Montage: 41.
Superstock International, Inc.: © M. & B. Reed, 13 (left), 65
(right).
Tony Stone Images: © James Strachan, 4; © Darrell Jones, 6;
© Kevin Schafer, 13 (right), 28; © K.Shafer/M Hill, 15; © Alain
Le Garsmeur, 68; © Paul Merideth, 74 (right).
Travel Stock: © Buddy Mays, 17 (right), 25 (top right), 30, 58
(center left and bottom right), 84 (left), 94, 97 (left).
UPI/Bettmann: 19, 47, 51 (left), 53 (right and left), 65 (left).
Valan Photos: © Tom W. Parkin, 20 (center left); © Albert
Kuhnigk, 20 (bottom right); © Ken Cole, 22 (right); 24 (right);
© Rob Simpson, 23 (top left); © Jeff Foott, 25 (top left);
© Marguerite Servais, 26; © John Cancalosi, 60, 102 (left);
© John Mitchell, 85; © Y.R. Tymstra, 106 (right).

Cover: Reflections on Collet Canal in Belize City

A rural house built of local wood and thatch from coconut palms

TABLE OF CONTENTS

A small boat approaches one of the many cays, or raised sandy islands, off the coast of Belize.

Chapter 1

THE ONE-OF-A-KIND COUNTRY

Belize, formerly known as British Honduras, is one of seven countries in Central America. It shares its borders with Mexico's Yucatán to the north and Guatemala to the west and south. In the east it borders the Caribbean Sea.

There are several possibilities for the origin of the name *Belize.* The most popular explanation associates it with a Scottish pirate, Peter Wallace, who was probably the first European to spend time there. The Spaniards pronounced his last name in a way that evolved into "Belize." But an alternative meaning may be "muddy waters," from a native Mayan word, *belix,* while a third suggestion gives the name an African derivation.

Geographically Belize shares many of the features of its Central American neighbors. It has rain forests and cloud forests, some small mountain ranges, and scrubland, as well as swamps and mangroves, but it has no volcanoes. Unique to Belize is the spectacular barrier reef that lies offshore and is the longest of its kind in the western hemisphere. Lying parallel to the coastline, the reef is fringed by many small islands known as *cays.*

Although Belize is part of Central America, its history has been

very different from the other Central American countries. The
Spaniards conquered and developed those other countries from
early in the sixteenth century, but they showed little interest in the
region of Belize. While they assumed it to be part of their colonial
possessions, they allowed logmen, mostly British, to cut trees for
shipment to Europe. The foundations were thus laid for a dispute
over ownership of the territory that has gone on into the twentieth
century, and which, even now, is not completely resolved.

British Honduras was declared a British Crown Colony in 1862
and became fully independent in 1981. With a weak economy, high
unemployment, and other problems common to developing

The harbor at Belize City, former capital of Belize, is home port to many small boats that belong to both tourists and working fishermen.

countries, it relies heavily on the United States for financial help and economic assistance.

The people of Belize are of widely mixed origins, many having arrived as laborers or as refugees. While a small number prefer to retain their own identity, the majority have developed a Belizean society in which the differing cultural and language traditions have been successfully merged together, with remarkably little racial tension.

A boy hopes to catch some fish in a marsh along a warm river in the interior of Belize.

Chapter 2

THE LAND

Belize is the second smallest country in Central America. Only El Salvador is smaller. Belize covers a territory of 8,866 square miles (22,962 square kilometers), approximately the size of the state of New Hampshire. From north to south, its greatest length is only 174 miles (280 kilometers), and its greatest width east to west is less than 70 miles (112 kilometers).

It is the least densely populated country in the region, with less than 22.5 persons per square mile (8.5 per square kilometer). By far the greatest concentration of people live in Belize City. This coastal city was the capital city until 1970. Following the devastation caused to the city by Hurricane Hattie in 1961, an entirely new capital, called Belmopan, was built in the interior 50 miles (80 kilometers) southwest of Belize City.

HIGHLANDS AND LOWLANDS

Underlying Belize is a mass of limestone, part of a vast area of ancient rock stretching from the Yucatán of Mexico in the north to Nicaragua in the south, and beneath the sea for about 20 miles (32.2 kilometers) away from the coast. Over millions of years, the rock has been raised and tilted by movements of the earth's crust. The tilt gives rise to elevated land in the south and west of Belize,

Punta Gorda is the southernmost town in Belize.

and to lower land in the north and east. The southern part of Belize is a plateau of forest-clad limestone hills. The most prominent of these hills are the Maya Mountains.

The Maya range extends roughly parallel to the coast and is separated from the sea by a coastal plain averaging 15 miles (24.1 kilometers) wide with an elevation of about 10 feet (3 meters). The principal towns of southern Belize are located on the coast. Punta Gorda, the most southerly, is fringed by palms. Placentia is smaller and close to Mango Creek. It is a banana-exporting port. Dangriga, once known as Stann Creek, is the largest town in the region. It is located at the mouth of a river set in a valley famed for its rich citrus fruit production. Dangriga is connected to the new capital, Belmopan, by a road that skirts the northern limit of the Maya Mountains. It passes through forested limestone country dotted with caves and waterfalls, including places where streams disappear into underground passages.

Even today, the Maya Mountains are not fully explored because they are hollowed with hundreds of caves. One of the biggest caves is at forested Rio Frio in the northwest of the range.

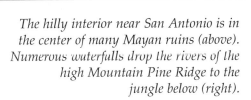

The hilly interior near San Antonio is in the center of many Mayan ruins (above). Numerous waterfulls drop the rivers of the high Mountain Pine Ridge to the jungle below (right).

One chamber of these caves is 525 feet (160 meters) long. A waterfall in the nearby Mountain Pine Ridge tumbles more than 1,000 feet (304 meters). At the northern end of the range on the seaward side, several isolated peaks rise as a series of irregular humps known as the Cockscomb Range. The tallest peak, Victoria, at 3,680 feet (1,122 meters), is the highest point in Belize.

The northern part of Belize seldom rises above 200 feet (61 meters). The highest land in the north is in the west, near the border with Guatemala, where steep escarpments flank the Rio Bravo and Booth's River. In other places, the land is often swampy and broken by lagoons filled with mangroves, tropical trees that support their crowns by sending roots from the trunk and into water.

A number of shallow ridges and hollows that run roughly north to south across this region were formed by coral reefs deposited on the rocky limestone base before it was raised from

13

English Cay (left), seen from above, is one of many small sandy islands formed on the remnants of a coral reef in very shallow water. The Blue Hole (right) is an underwater cave located in a lagoon in the middle of a coral atoll called Lighthouse Reef.

the sea. The ancient reefs would be hardly discernible now except that trees and other plants growing there vary according to the soils formed on the ridges and in the hollows. The main northern towns are Orange Walk, which is inland, and Corozal on the northern side of a bay close to the Mexican frontier.

BARRIER REEF AND CAYS

Offshore coral reefs are still being formed, and about 15 miles (24 kilometers) from the coast the coral has formed a beautiful string of islands known as the Cays, pronounced "kees." The word comes from the Spanish cayo, meaning "small island or reef." Many of the cays are uninhabited, but on Ambergris Cay in the north, the small town of San Pedro is now the center of a growing tourist industry.

The islands represent the line of an old reef that is gradually being lifted from the sea. Some are well above water and clad with coconut palms, while others—the "wet" cays—are partially submerged and covered by mangroves. A few miles out into the ocean, beyond the general line of cays, lies the barrier reef, which is an almost totally submerged ridge of coral reef. This reef,

teeming with marine life, extends from the southern tip of
Mexico's Yucatán for approximately 150 miles (240 kilometers).

Beyond the barrier reef are three coral atolls, formations
usually associated with the Indian and Pacific oceans. The largest
and most prominent Belizean atoll extends about 35 miles (56
kilometers) from north to south, with its own reefs, cays, and a
well-protected central lagoon. These formations together are
known as Turneffe Islands.

Twelve miles (19 kilometers) east of Turneffe lies Lighthouse
Reef, which has fewer cays but is renowned for its shallow lagoon
and famed Blue Hole. The depth of the lagoon varies from 5 to 15
feet (1.5 to 4.5 meters). Roughly in the middle of the lagoon is an
underwater hole with a diameter of about 450 feet (137 meters)
and depth of 340 feet (103.5 meters). At the 140-foot (42.5-meter)
level, the hole opens into a spectacular cavern complete with

gigantic stalactites hanging from the limestone roof as if it were out on dry land.

A third atoll, Glover's Reef, lies approximately 12 miles (19 kilometers) south of the other two and encloses a beautiful lagoon dotted with patches of coral. Together the cays and islands along the Belizean coast account for approximately 212 square miles (547 square kilometers) or 2.4 percent of the country.

RIVERS

The northern part of Belize is drained by two rivers, the Hondo, which marks the border with Mexico and flows into the Bay of Chetumal, and the New River. The New River enters the same bay after a long course meandering northward. This meander is broken in one place by the 15-mile (24-kilometer) New River Lagoon. This river has long been used by lumbermen to transport their products to the coast via the town of Orange Walk.

The Belize River rises in the low-lying Petén region of neighboring Guatemala, where it is known as the Rio Mopán. It enters Belize near the border town of Benque Viejo, 81 miles (130 kilometers) from Belize City. The eastern branch of the Belize River, called River Macal, rises in the Maya Mountains and flows between the towns of San Ignacio and Santa Elena. The Belize River is navigable for many miles inland from the sea and has traditionally been the route for transporting produce from the interior. The river has deposited large quantities of silt at its mouth, forming a delta, much of which is now reclaimed land. The river enters the sea about 5 miles (8 kilometers) north of Belize City. One branch of the river, known as Haulover Creek, passes through

The New River (left) has long been a working river; here it is being used to load and transport sugarcane. The Belize River (right) runs through dense jungle.

the town. At one time, cattle were hauled over the creek on ropes.

Heavy rainfall in the Maya Mountains feeds countless small rivers, such as Monkey River, but most of them have short courses. Only those flowing north have space to grow, and from the heights of Mountain Pine Ridge, some tributaries tumble over falls and through ravines to the Belize River. Others fall into the Sibun River, which enters the sea less than 10 miles (16 kilometers) south of Belize City. Many short rivers from the southern flank of the Maya Mountains, such as the Temash and Moho, empty into the Gulf of Honduras. The longest river in this region is the Sarstoon, which rises in the highlands of the interior of Guatemala and forms Belize's southern border.

CLIMATE

For much of the year, the climate in Belize is subtropical with trade winds from the Caribbean moderating the temperatures along the coast. In Belize City, the temperature in the shade seldom exceeds 90° Fahrenheit (32° Celsius). Sometimes between November and February, the temperature can be as low as 55° F

A storm is seen brewing from Line Cay, in the barrier reef off Belize.

(13° C) when cold frontal storms known as "northers" blow across the sea from the chilled landmass of North America. Often these periods of cold weather are followed by days of wind and rain, accompanied by *chubascos*, or thundery storms. Away from the coast, the temperatures can exceed 100° F (38° C).

Belize has a well-defined dry season from February to April and a wet season from June to October, although the amount of rain may vary from year to year and from north to south of the country. The north is drier and may even sometimes have droughts. In the south, the rainfall may average 180 inches (458 centimeters).

While the climate is mostly predictable, the Belizeans have grown to expect some unusual conditions. They know a period of dry, calm weather in August as the "mauger season" when, for a week or two, the heat is oppressive and insects, mainly from the swamps, are troublesome. The "hurricane season" follows, usually from September to November, though in some years it starts as early as June.

In the past fifty years, hurricanes have twice brought devastation. Corozal was struck by Hurricane Janet in 1955. Then, in 1961,

Hurricane Hattie struck Belize City on October 31, 1961, destroying about 85 percent of the city. This picture was taken the next day.

Belize City was virtually destroyed by Hurricane Hattie when winds reached 150 miles per hour (240 kilometers per hour) and a wind-blown wave 14 feet (4.3 meters) high raced in from the sea. Previously, Belize City was struck by other hurricanes and, though records are far from reliable, the hurricanes of 1787, 1931, and 1942 are considered to have killed the most people. In 1931, some 2,500 people died in one day. Others hurricanes have caused millions of dollars' worth of damage to crops. Hurricane Greta in 1978, for example, brought two weeks of continuous rain and heavy floods.

PLANT LIFE

Much of Belize used to be covered by forest except for places in the southern coastal and central northern regions where open grasslands, called savannas, contain only a few, scattered trees. Over the past 300 years, loggers and farmers have changed the

Some of the plants that add to the spectacle of Belize (clockwise from bottom right): red mangroves, which send out aerial roots on which new land forms; heliconia, or lobster claw, flowers in the rain forest; a bromeliad from the cloud forest; an orchid, which is the Belizean national flower; a river running through the rain forest, seen through hibiscus flowers.

The savannas are areas of open grassland that occur only a few places in Belize.

face of forested areas near the coast and rivers, while elsewhere, especially in places away from roads, the vegetation remains untouched. Forests in the north contain mostly broadleaf, deciduous trees. Rivers there are bordered with a dense, often swampy growth. Mangrove forests fringe the northern coast, parts of the southern coast, and creek inlets.

Palm forests, largely of the majestic cohune palms, grow on the drier clay soils. In centuries past, these palms had considerable economic importance for the Maya. Places with sandy soils are covered with coniferous forests of Caribbean pine mixed with oak, and the higher parts of the Mountain Pine Ridge are clothed with a tall pine similar to pitch pine. The Maya Mountains with their height and rainfall are richly cloaked with a cloud forest, a leafy wilderness filled with ferns, bromeliads, and masses of orchids.

BIRDS

Because of its rich variety of habitats, Belize is home to many species of birds. The forest especially conceals an extraordinary number of species. Tiny hummingbirds dart from flower to flower.

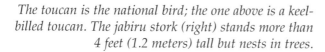
The toucan is the national bird; the one above is a keel-billed toucan. The jabiru stork (right) stands more than 4 feet (1.2 meters) tall but nests in trees.

Larger birds include the toucans with massive bills and bobbing flight and the brilliant macaws and other parrots. The toucan is the national bird. Belizean birds' ways of life vary considerably from that of the partridge-like ground-hugging tinamous to the massive jabiru stork. One of the largest flying birds in the Americas, this stork builds its nesting platform of twigs and other wood in trees high above the ground following the wet season.

Lagoons, riverbanks, and shores are home to many waterbirds and waders, among them the boat-billed heron, which uses its curious bill to scoop its food. Another remarkable bird is the snake bird, or anhinga, with an elegantly long neck and long bill. Other waterbirds include many species of ducks, egrets, including the cattle egret, grebes, bitterns, kingfishers, and white ibis, as well as delicately colored roseate spoonbills, which feed on small crustaceans, insects, and other water life.

The birds of the coast and cays include several terns, gulls, and the magnificent frigatebirds—also called man-of-war birds—which often stay close to the red-footed boobies nesting on Half Moon Cay at the southeastern end of Lighthouse Reef.

More birds of Belize include (clockwise from left): the king vulture, the most colorful vulture in the world; the anhinga, which is also called the snake bird, because of the way its thin neck looks as the bird swims, and the American darter; the red-footed booby (shown with a chick) is a long-distance flier; and the magnificent frigatebird, shown with its throat sac expanded during courtship, also called the man-of-war bird. The booby and the frigatebird are coastal birds that fly long distances out over the ocean before returning to Belize to nest.

OTHER ANIMALS

Much of the Belizean animal life belongs to families strongly represented throughout Central and South America. The country's national animal is the tapir, about the size of a small cow, with short legs and a very mobile proboscis that it uses for browsing. Tapirs are often difficult to find in the wild as they keep to the

The jaguar (left) is the largest American member of the cat family. It swims in the rivers and marshes of Belize. The endangered margay (above) is much smaller and lives primarily in trees, where it eats birds, small mammals, and lizards.

undergrowth near streams and readily take to the water to escape predators such as jaguars, which also occur in Belize.

Jaguars, the largest American members of the cat family, can weigh as much as 300 pounds (136 kilograms). They hunt smaller animals such as small deer and wild forest pigs called peccaries, as well as a variety of rodents, including the large agoutis and pacas that browse on the forest floor. The pacas, their brown fur dappled with white spots, can reach almost 30 inches (76 centimeters) in length.

Of the other carnivores, the puma (cougar), margay, and ocelot are catlike, but another member of the cat family, the jaguarundi, has a long, otterlike body, short legs, a long tail, and small rounded ears. It is a good hunter and seeks out many of the forest's smaller mammals, young birds, frogs, and insects. Other carnivores include the raccoonlike coatimundis, which are sometimes kept as pets, and kinkajous, which are skillful climbers.

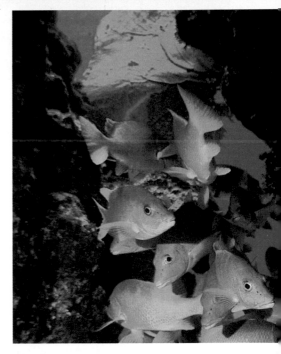

The tapir (above), the national mammal of Belize, is a piglike animal that lives in the forests. Also resident in the rain forests is the blue morpho butterfly (top right). Off the coast are many rocky reefs that support such fish as these colorful grunts (right).

The favorite Belizean monkey, which is now rare, is the black howler monkey, often given the Creole name of "baboon." True baboons are African while the howler monkeys live only in South and Central America. They get their name from their curiously enlarged bony voice box. By forcing air across the hyoid bone in the larynx, a howler makes its booming noise heard throughout the forest.

Another unusual animal, also rare in Belize, is the manatee, or sea cow. This large, gentle mammal lives in the warm water of the rivers and bays, browsing on aquatic vegetation and growing to about 14 feet (4.3 meters) long.

Among the reptiles there are some dangerous snakes, particularly the fer-de-lance, a venomous pit viper, known locally as the yellow-jawed Tommy Goff. Other snakes with bad reputations, though not so aggressive, are coral snakes, banded black, yellow,

The seriously endangered black howler monkey, whose booming calls sound through the rain forest, is protected in a sanctuary at Bermudian Landing.

and red. Their venom is highly toxic and a strike is often fatal. Of the many lizards, the iguanas reaching about 3 feet (91 centimeters) long are the largest and can be seen in most country places, where they often serve as food.

Warm rivers emerging from tropical forests and the incredible biodiversity of the reefs support many different species of fish. From the catfish scavenging the bottoms of the rivers to the barracudas, tarpon, and groupers in the sea to the butterfly fish, grunts, damselfish, and sergeant majors (a type of damselfish) among the dozens of brilliantly colored species of the reef, Belize is richly endowed with fish. This bounty makes it a popular place for snorkeling.

NATIONAL PARKS AND RESERVES

The Belizeans have begun to develop a series of reserves where wildlife in all its forms is protected. One of the best known is

Guanacaste Park, a 50-acre (20-hectare) tropical forest just north of Belmopan. It is named after the guanacaste tree, which can reach a diameter of over 6 feet (1.8 meters) and a height of 130 feet (40 meters). Crooked Tree Wildlife Sanctuary is a network of lagoons, swamps, and waterways about 33 miles (53 kilometers) northwest of Belize City, noted for its abundant bird life.

Howler monkeys are protected in the Community Baboon Sanctuary at Bermudian Landing in the riverside forests of the Belize River. Eight local communities with rights to the land are involved and the project is supported by the Belizean Audubon Society as well as other international and American bodies.

Mountain Pine Ridge in the Maya Mountains is about 300 square miles (774 square kilometers) of protected land. Cockscomb Basin Jaguar Preserve at the foot of the high mountains near Dangriga is 150 square miles (388 square kilometers) of tropical forest set aside to protect jaguars, the first such reserve in the world.

Perhaps the most famous reserves of all are those along the reefs, such as Blue Hole National Park. Half Moon Cay National Monument protects nesting red-footed boobies. Hol Chan Marine Preserve at the southern end of Ambergris Cay is a popular diving destination. (*Hol Chan* means "little channel" in Mayan.) The barrier reef itself is called unique in the western hemisphere by the United Nations because of its untouched condition and its many sponges, corals, and fish.

NATURAL RESOURCES

To date, no significant mineral resources have been found in Belize, although exploration for oil and gas has continued for

This rain forest has been burned so that a banana plantation can be planted. If Belize is to achieve its potential, such land must be kept for the forest products it can produce.

some years. A hydroelectric dam has been built to supply energy, but much of the country's power is supplied by Mexico.

Traditionally, the country's main resource has been its forests, where quantities of logwood, mahogany, and other hardwoods have been felled for the United States and European furniture markets. Although the supply of these hardwoods has been considerably reduced, large tracts of forests still represent a valuable natural resource, and not just for felled timber. There is a good deal of interest in the market for forest products, which could be developed without destroying the trees. These products include medicinal plants, orchids, chicle used for making chewing gum, rubber, orchids, natural oils, and nuts. It will take time to develop these products and make them economic. In the meantime, Belize's main resources are its agricultural land and the development of areas suitable for growing sugar and citrus fruits.

Belize has a good resource in fish, for both commercial and tourist exploitation. But already there are warning signs that if the

Eco-tourists on the Macal River enter the rain forest quietly and respectfully.

supply is not carefully controlled, it will soon disappear. Lobster and conch are very popular and continue to be caught even in the off-season when fishing is officially prohibited.

BELIZE'S POTENTIAL

Although Belize did not achieve independence until 1981, it has already proved to be a democratic and stable country in a region torn apart by civil war and revolution. Considerable effort has and is being made to expand the economy and diversify the means by which the country can balance its budget. Though Belize still relies heavily on foreign aid, it owes less money to other governments and banks than do many other developing countries.

Its most exciting potential lies with the development of its forest, and with eco-tourism. Belize now considers its nature reserves as a major resource, and the flow of eco-tourists is increasing yearly. If the true potential of such tourism is to be realized, care will have to be taken to maintain a balance between the number of visitors and the possible harm they can do to the environment.

The Temple to the Sun God was found in the excavated Mayan city of Altún Ha, in the Belize jungle. The temple was built during the Classic period for the 8,000 to 10,000 residents of the area.

Chapter 3

LAND OF THE BAYMEN

Centuries before the arrival of the Spaniards in Mexico and Central America, several great native American civilizations inhabited the region. Although the Aztecs are perhaps the best known, the Maya, whose territory included Mexico's Yucatán, Guatemala's Petén, and parts of Honduras and Belize, are considered the most advanced.

Archeologists divide the Mayan civilization into three periods: the Formative (1200 B.C. to A.D. 300), the Classic (A.D. 300 to 900), and the Interregnum (A.D. 900 to 1000). Based on recent digs in Cuello in Belize, some archeologists place the beginning of the Mayan civilization at more than 4,000 years ago.

The Formative period covers the years of development, when the Maya, together with other groups of people, were semi-nomadic hunters. Like their ancestors, they lived off fish, animals of the forest, and seeds and nuts. Gradually they settled into communities, built huts of thatch, made simple pots, and cleared patches of forest to grow crops. They learned to cultivate corn, cotton, beans, squash, chili peppers, and such fruits as avocado and papaya. Some ceremonial centers were built, which served as the bases for the huge pyramids and temples still seen today.

The Maya were at their greatest during the Classic period, particularly in the lowland forests of southern Mexico, Guatemala,

Archeologists continue to discover more buried remains of early Mayan civilizations. This archeologist was working in a royal burial tomb he discovered in 1986. Inset is a small clay pot, one of the artifacts found in the tomb.

and Belize. However, theirs was not one vast unified nation. Instead, they lived in a series of independent city-states ruled by priests and nobles. Each city-state vied with the others in the grandeur of its temples, pyramids, and palaces. Trade among the city-states moved fish, shells, and pottery from the coast, and obsidian, jade, and copper from the interior.

The greatest of all the cities, with a population of over 10,000 people, was Tikal in Guatemala. The center of the city covered an area of about 6 square miles (15.5 square kilometers) and contained about 3,000 buildings. The peasant farming community, located beyond the main city, had its own major and minor ceremonial centers of which there are several in Belize, including Xunantunich and Altún Ha.

Not only were the Maya skilled builders, but they were also accomplished scientists, astronomers, artists, and potters. They developed a form of *glyph*, a system of writing that used symbols.

The "ballgame" was probably used both for recreation and as a means of selecting human sacrifices for religious ceremonies. The narrow court used for the game was probably similar to this one at Tikal in Guatemala.

They carved this writing on stone slabs, or *stelae,* which they gathered into a *codex.* Unfortunately, many of these collections, or *codices,* were destroyed by the Spaniards, but the stelae still exist. From the glyphs, experts have worked out details of Mayan history and learned of their advanced knowledge of mathematics. Significantly, the Maya had discovered the use of the arithmetical zero. They also devised a calendar system based on a year of 365 days, long before one was used in Europe.

For relaxation, the Mayas enjoyed the "ballgame," which was played on a large court, often with sloping wall sides. The object was to get a rubber ball through a carved stone ring high on the wall. As players could use only fists, elbows, or buttocks to hit the ball, this was far from easy.

The Interregnum period marks the time when the Maya, for reasons which are not clear, migrated north from Belize into Mexico's Yucatán, abandoning their homes, farms, and ceremonial centers. There is speculation that the people moved to escape warfare between the city-states. Whatever the reason, by the time the Europeans arrived, much of Belize was uninhabited.

PIRATES AND BAYMEN

Christopher Columbus may have sighted the coast of Belize on his fourth and last voyage to the Americas in 1502. But the Spanish sailors and explorers who followed made few attempts to settle there. It was an inhospitable region of swamps and mangroves, but, more importantly, it did not have the gold or other minerals for which they were searching.

The Bay of Honduras, the cays, and the coast did, however, become well known to British and other pirates seeking to capture the Spanish galleons taking treasure from other parts of the Americas back to Spain. It is thought that the first pirate to set up camp near the Belize River was a former lieutenant of Walter Raleigh, Peter Wallace, in 1603.

Some years later, in 1638, a group of shipwrecked English sailors took refuge there, and Belize City dates its founding from their settlement. These sailors were joined by people from the island of Jamaica, while pirates from several nations increasingly used the cays to attack the Spanish flotilla. Among the more infamous pirates working in the region were Captain William Kidd, Blackbeard (Edward Teach), and Sir Henry Morgan. The British government did little to stop them.

Pirates and settlers alike quickly realized that while Belize may not have had gold, it did have logwood. This tropical wood was highly valued by furniture makers in Britain and Europe for its red

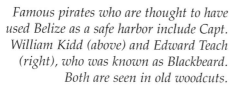

Famous pirates who are thought to have used Belize as a safe harbor include Capt. William Kidd (above) and Edward Teach (right), who was known as Blackbeard. Both are seen in old woodcuts.

color, and cutting these trees soon became a profitable business. Many of the people living around the Bay of Honduras, known as the Baymen, became loggers, working with some native people of the Mosquito tribe from the south, as well as English and Scottish settlers who came to hear of the new industry.

By 1670 the population of the Bay Settlement had reached 700. The British governor of Jamaica, some 600 miles (960 kilometers) away, who kept an eye on affairs of Belize, urged the British government to declare it a colony. However, the British, fearing Spanish retaliation, did nothing. Instead, a treaty between the two nations in 1670 gave the Baymen Spanish permission to continue cutting logwood, but it left the question of who owned the land unclear.

The Spaniards tried to control the trading of logwood by insisting that only Spanish ships could carry the product. Even so, the Baymen, who were beginning to assert some independence and demand legal rights, managed to develop a trade with the United States. A major conflict being fought in Europe ended in 1713 with the Treaty of Utrecht. Among the bargaining points were the main powers' colonies in the New World. The Spaniards were forced to relinquish their monopoly on carrying goods to and from Spanish America, including Belize. The South Sea Company, a private British firm, was granted the right to carry some goods and to supply the Spanish colonies with some black African slaves.

Thousands of the native Amerindian population had died of diseases introduced by the Europeans and because of the severe conditions in which they were forced to work for the settlers. As a result, there was a shortage of laborers in most parts of Central and South America. Black slaves from Africa and the Caribbean were welcomed when they began to arrive in the Bay Settlement in 1720. The slaves quickly became an important part of the community as the Baymen came to depend on them.

THE SPANISH CONFLICT

During most of the eighteenth century, the Baymen of Belize were involved in skirmishes with the Spaniards. In 1718 a small army of Spanish and Indian soldiers entered Belize from the Guatemalan Petén. Faced with fierce resistance from the loggers, they could do no more than build a fort on Belize River near Spanish Lookout, and eventually they left. Meanwhile, the newly appointed Spanish governor of the Yucatán in Mexico had orders to stop the logging and make the men work in the Mexican mines. In 1733, on his instructions, a Spanish fleet with some 700 men set

This tall Spanish cedar is typical of the giant hardwood trees that were cut and exported from the forests of Belize during the early centuries of the country's occupation by Europeans.

out for Belize and succeeded in demolishing most of the Bay Settlement. But the loggers soon rebuilt their town.

Belize was again attacked in 1739 as the result of a war between England and Spain. Several logging camps were destroyed, and Belize City was threatened once again. Despite appeals from the loggers, the British government still would not recognize the Bay Settlement as a colony. Nor were the loggers legally allowed to build fortifications. Even so, in 1754 some 250 loggers won a notable victory by defeating a Spanish force of more than 1,500 men from Guatemala.

But there was a limit to the patience of the courageous loggers. They decided that, despite British government objections, they would engage an engineer to help them build a fort at the entrance to Belize City. The fort had a short life, however, because the British government agreed in the Treaty of Paris in 1763 to destroy it. In return, the Spaniards extended the settlers' rights to work and trade logwood. But no mention was made of mahogany, a severe disappointment to the settlers.

In 1764 the British government appointed a person to formalize a system of self-government for the Settlement, but hostilities with the Spaniards continued for almost another twenty years, until the Treaty of Versailles in 1783. Partly as a result of the American Revolution (1776 to 1783), the first American families emigrated to the Bay Settlement. In the Treaty of Versailles, Spain granted the settlers some concessions, including the trade in mahogany but at a cost. Britain had to agree not to establish any colonial government except "that necessary to maintain law and order." Within months, though, the British government appointed, at the request of the settlers, its first Superintendent to oversee the affairs of the territory.

By 1796 England and Spain were again at war. Once again, the Spanish governor of the Yucatán sent a Spanish force of over thirty ships and 2,500 men. The people of Belize, determined to protect their settlement, repulsed the Spaniards several times. The final encounter came on September 10, 1798, when the combined forces of the Spanish fleet attacked St. George's Cay, only to be repulsed once again by the loggers and their friends. This was the last attempt made by the Spaniards to take Belize by force, and September 10 is celebrated every year as a Belizean national holiday. The victory is also seen by many as the basis of Britain's claim to sovereignty over Belize.

CENTRAL AMERICAN FEDERATION

Early in the nineteenth century, Spain was heavily involved with the Napoleonic Wars in Europe and could no longer devote attention to its colonies in Spanish America. Mexico declared its independence from Spain in 1821, followed soon after by the other

The harbor of Belize when it became British Honduras

THE TREATY OF 1859

In 1859 Guatemala and Britain agreed to try and resolve their claims over Belize. The United States was taking an interest in the affairs of Central America, and both Guatemala and Britain were anxious to resolve the dispute without further complications. In exchange for Guatemala's recognition of the existing boundaries of Belize, Britian agreed to build a road to connect the Guatemalan capital with the Settlement of Belize. The road, which would have to be carved through forests and over some mountains, would be costly. Ultimately, the British government decided that the road would be too costly and might threaten Belize's commerce rather than enhance trade between the two countries. The road, never built, has been the cause of dispute between the two countries ever since. Guatemala, insisting that the terms of the treaty were not fulfilled, has regularly reinstated its claim to Belize.

In 1862, following repeated requests from the people and local government in Belize, Britain finally agreed that Belize should become a colony. It was to be known as British Honduras.

Government House in Belize City (above) was the residence of the colonial governor of the country until independence.

The National Assembly Building (below) is the centerpiece of the new capital development in Belmopan.

Chapter 4

THE MAKING OF
A NATION

British Honduras became a Crown Colony in 1871. It was administered by a governor appointed by the British Crown. The colonists had mixed feelings about the situation. It could be a welcome step toward eventual independence, but it meant that they had to give up local government, which many colonists resented. Also unfortunate was the fact that most of the governors appointed to the colony during the next half century either were disinterested in their job or had their own commercial interests in the land. Often they considered these interests more important than helping to improve the conditions of the ordinary people.

When it became a colony, British Honduras's economic situation was not good. The Spaniards, while allowing the Baymen to cut and trade wood, had always forbidden them to cultivate the land. As a result, the country had no agricultural base, and most of its food had to be imported. During the nineteenth century, sugar, and later bananas, were cultivated but only by a few wealthy landowners and large companies who controlled most of the land. One company formed in 1859, and later known as the Belize Estate and Produce Company, came to own one-fifth of the entire country. There was a temporary respite in the 1860s when the Belizeans made good profits by supplying the two sides of the American Civil War with guns, ammunition, and other contraband. But a scheme to bring in people from the American South to grow cotton did not work.

Toward the end of the nineteenth century, much of the country was still unknown. Several expeditions explored toward the Guatemalan border, into the Maya and Cockscomb mountain ranges, through the Stann Creek District, and up the Sibun River. Though some mineral resources were located, they were difficult to find again because proper maps had never been made.

There were no real roads—just a few dirt trails—no wheeled transport, and no railroads. Most goods were transported by horse and cart or by river. Mail boats piled high with foodstuffs, animals, and household goods made a regular journey from Belize City to the north. Apart from sloops and paddle steamers, there were also craft resembling the original Mayan flat-bottomed canoes called *pit-pans.* One report describes the governor's pit-pan as a familiar sight on the Belize River. It was 40 feet (12 meters) long, 6 feet (1.8 meters) wide, and carved out of a single mahogany log. Furnished with drapes and cushions and manned by soldiers in red and gold uniforms, it resembled a fancy Venetian gondola.

INTO THE TWENTIETH CENTURY

The beginning of the twentieth century saw some modest improvements. In Belize City, street lighting was introduced, some lighthouses were constructed to help shipping, and the Bank of British Honduras was founded. More importantly, telephone lines

Mahogany sawmills such as this one were an important activity during the early part of the colonial era. Only the energy source for running the big saw is different now.

were constructed linking Belize City with the north and south of the country. This was a vital step in bridging the gap between city and rural dwellers. For the most part, rural inhabitants had been ignored, while Belize City developed as the hub of the country's commercial and political life. Everything of importance was centered in the city, including the few educational and medical facilities.

Although a short-lived railroad was built south of Belize City near Stann Creek, road building was ignored. The timber merchants, whose profits were tied to shipping on the river, resisted the construction of roads through the countryside. Most rural areas had no contact with Belize City by road until after 1930.

Forestry was still the major economic activity in the colony. Mahogany had replaced logwood as the most important product, and together with other hardwoods represented over three-quarters of the country's exports. But as mahogany trees became harder to locate, loggers had to search deeper into the forests, and many were working beyond the colony's boundaries. In the 1920s, experiments conducted by a new Forestry Department in a special reserve showed that it was possible to replace and restock mahogany using properly controlled methods. This gave the industry a new lease of life.

The forestry industry also produced chicle, which was used to make chewing gum, for which there was great demand in the United States. Gatherers collect chicle from the sapodilla tree by climbing high up the trunk and slashing the bark so that the sap runs down into a cup.

For the first time, serious attention was paid to the agricultural industry. A sugar factory was established, owned jointly by private planters and the government, and the promotion of a Belizean rum was encouraged. The production of bananas, which had been introduced late in the nineteenth century by American and British investors, proved more difficult. Although the land and climate were suitable, plantations were hit on several occasions by disease, and hurricanes, such as that in 1931, devastated the harvest. Other crops included rice, coffee, tobacco, tropical fruits, and rubber.

The agricultural industry always faced the two problems of labor and land. The people of British Honduras were traditionally loggers and did not see themselves as farmers. And they regarded plantation workers as having a rather inferior status associated with workers in the Caribbean. The small farmer found land difficult to get and difficult to keep. In the early 1900s, over one-third of the colony was owned by just one foreign company, and, like other landowners, it preferred to make its profits from the well-tried timber industry.

Another problem arose as a consequence of the hurricane in 1931. The devastation had been immense and there was no way that Belizeans could rebuild the colony without financial help from the British government. Great Britain agreed to a loan but, in

The hurricane of 1931 destroyed the Belizeans' moves toward independence as well as major cities and agricultural crops.

return, insisted that the governor and a new Legislative Council take control of the colony's finances until the loan was paid off. But the colony found repayment impossible. Britain would not allow the council to change its outdated tax system or to increase the taxes paid by the mostly British-owned big businesses.

An apparently unbreakable circle was established—the colony could not pay its debts because it was under British control, and it remained under British control because it could not pay its debts.

TOWARD SELF-GOVERNMENT

The first stirring of anticolonial feeling began among Creoles, who were descendants of African-European marriages. Creole soldiers fought in World War I alongside many nationalities. When they returned home to British Honduras, they resented being forced back into apparent second-class status, and in 1919 riots broke out. In the 1920s and 1930s, organizations and labor movements that were started to promote the nationalistic cause attracted many of the returning soldiers.

George Cadle Price, often called the "Father of Belize," helped form the first political party to oppose British policies. He and his colleagues founded the People's United Party, and he became the first prime minister.

The end of the Second World War brought more dissatisfaction. Many Belizeans who had fought alongside the British, Europeans, and, later, Americans returned home to find they had no job and no security. At the same time, there were many among the middle and upper classes who wanted greater freedom to run their businesses. They resented the financial conditions imposed by the British government.

The two groups came together when the British Honduran dollar was devalued in 1949, cutting the value of the local currency almost by half. The devaluation was completely beyond the control of the Belizeans, and was badly handled by the British government who had promised it would not happen. Because many of British Honduras's imports came from the United States, Belizeans suddenly had to pay much more for basic food and goods. The poor particularly were badly hit.

A People's Committee was formed to oppose the devaluation. The committee, which later became the People's United Party (PUP), was led by George Cadle Price and Philip Goldson, who, together with other members of the group, had been students at St. John's College in Belize City. There they had been taught by American Jesuit priests with strong views on Catholicism and socialism. In 1950, the PUP entered the elections for the City

Council, with a policy calling for the end of colonial rule, and won. From the outset, the British government, suspicious of the PUP, made things difficult for the young party. On one occasion, it dissolved the City Council because the members refused to hang a picture of Queen Elizabeth II in City Hall.

Because only those people with a certain level of income and land could vote, in 1945 there were only 822 registered voters in the whole of British Honduras. An important demand of the PUP was that everyone should have the right to vote. In 1954 the British government gave in partway, and provided a constitution that gave the right to vote to all adults who could read and write.

The new constitution also established a new Legislative Assembly, composed of some elected and some appointed members. George Price and his colleagues determined to campaign throughout the country, and, despite some infighting in their own party and attempts to discredit them, the PUP won eight out of nine elected seats in the Assembly. They picked up the ninth seat in the next elections, three years later.

Reforms to the Legislative Assembly in 1960 allowed for more elected members, and the 1961 elections returned the PUP with a full house of all eighteen elected members. Two years later, First Minister George Price was in London to discuss a new constitution that would give British Honduras full self-government. It came into effect on January 1, 1964. A National Assembly was created with a House of Representatives of elected members and a Senate with members appointed by the governor and the political parties. The British Government retained responsibility for national defense and foreign affairs. British Honduras officially took the name *Belize* in June 1973.

THE GUATEMALA QUESTION

The dispute between Great Britain and Guatemala has rumbled on throughout this century. It was revived in the 1930s when the British government tried to arrange a joint survey of the border between the two countries. The work was through unexplored, unhealthy jungle, and local engineers were employed because they were considered better able to cope with the conditions than the British Royal Engineers. The Guatemalans did not join in but kept a watchful eye on the operation.

Once the survey was complete, the Guatemalans were asked to agree with the border line that had been demarcated. They refused, citing once again the unfinished business of the 1859 Treaty, when Great Britain had not built the road that had been promised. Instead, they offered to buy the colony for a sum of money, at the same time releasing Great Britain from its 1859 obligations. A curt reply from the British government indicated there was no point in further talks. There the matter rested until after World War II. In 1945, in a new constitution, Guatemala referred to Belize as the twenty-third department of the country.

When Belize became self-governing in 1964, Guatemala made an immediate protest. It broke off diplomatic relations with Britain and hinted at war. Clearly, the Guatemala question would have to be resolved before Belize could become a wholly independent nation. Negotiations were resumed, but as the British government was responsible for Belizean foreign affairs, no representatives from Belize could take part. It was agreed in 1965 that the United States should appoint an attorney to act as mediator. After three years of investigation, he suggested that Belize should become

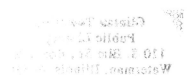

A British Royal Air Force missile-armed Harrier jet (above) is being worked on at Belize International Airport in 1975, when Britain sent the RAF to Belize as a warning to Guatemala not to invade. This British soldier (right) was stationed in Belize in 1982. Since then, most British troops have been withdrawn.

independent but effectively be under the control of the Guatemalan government. That proposal was resoundedly rejected by both parties.

Further negotiations, begun in 1969, ended three years later with Guatemala, helped by El Salvador, threatening to invade Belize. The British government sent a large number of troops to defend the territory and the war rumbles stopped. Talks began again in 1976, by which time Belize was adopting a policy of gathering international support for its independence, through such bodies as the United Nations and the Organization of American States. Several resolutions were passed in the UN, each getting Belize closer to its goal, while Guatemala persisted in its claim. Britain and the United States suggested that Belize could cede some of its territory in return for a settlement with Guatemala, but Belize held out against these proposals. Instead, it wanted the British government to deploy troops in Belize on a long-term basis as a deterrent to any possible invasion by Guatemala. In 1980 Belize, with the backing of the United States, won an important resolution in the United Nations, which virtually guaranteed independence.

In March 1981, Britain, Guatemala, and Belize signed a preliminary "Heads of Agreement" document. Guatemala would drop its claims and accept Belize's independence in return for access to the open sea through Belizean waters, and the right to build a road and an oil pipeline across Belizean territory. There were violent reaction to these proposals in both countries, and negotiations broke down a few months later. Nonetheless, Belize became independent on September 21, 1981, having received a guarantee from the British government that it would station troops there, at least for a limited period.

AN INDEPENDENT NATION

George Price and his People's United Party have been dominant in Belizean politics since the 1950s. Having successfully brought the country to full independence, however, they found new problems to consider. A priority has been to determine where Belize's allegiances should lie. A member of the Commonwealth of Nations, there is no question about loyalty to the British Crown, but in its people, society, and culture, Belize has assocations with both the West Indies and the Central American republics. In addition, Belize lies in the American sphere of influence. For many years, and particularly soon after independence, it has received much financial, economic, and military aid from the United States. Belize's economy has also been very tied to the United States.

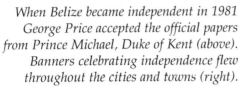

*When Belize became independent in 1981
George Price accepted the official papers
from Prince Michael, Duke of Kent (above).
Banners celebrating independence flew
throughout the cities and towns (right).*

Splits in the PUP between the pro-U.S. faction and the left, who favored Cuba and communism, together with another downturn in the economy, cost George Price the 1984 election. For the first time, the opposition United Democratic Party (UDP), led by Manuel Esquivel, came to power. The party was strongly pro-United States and, during its tenure of office, U.S. assistance reached record levels.

Belize's economy also strengthened in the late 1980s, with sugar and other agricultural products fetching high prices on the international market. Coming shortly before the elections in 1989, it was perhaps not coincidental that the UDP government, helped by international funds, invested heavily in much-needed roads, bridges, and telecommunications. They also completed the international airport and began a new hospital in Belize City. Contrary to expectations, these moves did not win them the election, however, and the PUP was returned to power in 1989.

Belizeans voted in their first election in 1984 (above). At that time, they chose Manuel Esquivel (right) to be prime minister, though George Price later regained the position.

During the years since independence, the Guatemala question has never been far out of sight. A solution seemed imminent in 1990, and it was a good sign for Belize when, with Guatemalan approval, it was invited to join the Organization of American States. The breakthrough appeared to come in 1991 when Prime Minister George Price reached a historic agreement with President Jorge Serrano of Guatemala. However, the agreement had still not been ratified two years later when President Serrano was removed from office. He was accused of treason for having reached this agreement without first holding a referendum—a public-opinion vote required by the Guatemalan constitution.

Even so, a month later, Serrano's successor, President Ramiro Carpio, gave the agreement his backing. In the meantime, George Price lost the 1993 election, largely because of the uncertainty surrounding these events and an indication by the British government that it would be withdrawing its troops. Esquivel also accused Price of giving away Belizean citizenship and voting rights to thousands of refugees from other parts of Central America, and of selling passports to Chinese nationals from Hong Kong as a means of helping them get into the United States.

Prime Minister Esquivel tried, but failed, to persuade the British government not to remove the troops from Belize. All were withdrawn except a hundred or so who have remained to organize training for jungle warfare. The hope is that the long-standing dispute between Guatemala and Belize has now, finally, come to an end, but it may be years before Belizeans will feel entirely safe.

GOVERNMENT

Belize's government is based on the constitution passed on September 20, 1981, the day before the country became independent. It is a constitutional monarchy, with Queen Elizabeth II as head of state, and a form of government similar to that in Great Britain. The British sovereign is represented by the governor general, who is appointed on the advice of the prime minister and must be of Belizean nationality.

Executive authority lies with the governor general, the prime minister, and the cabinet of ministers. The prime minister is appointed by the governor general, and together they appoint a cabinet of ministers. Both the prime minister and the cabinet come from the majority party in the National Assembly.

The National Assembly is made up of two houses: the Senate, with eight appointed members, and the House of Representatives, with twenty-eight elected members. Senators are appointed by the

Independence Plaza in Belmopan is a new square of government buildings.

governor general, five on the advice of the prime minister, two on the advice of the leader of the opposition party, and one after consultation with the Belize Advisory Council. Members of the House of Representatives are elected by all adults over the age of eighteen, and they represent the twenty-eight constituencies into which the country is divided for electoral purposes. Legislative power is vested in the National Assembly, which must approve all new laws. The term of office for senators and representatives is normally five years.

The Belize Advisory Council is made up of at least six people "of integrity and high national standing." They are appointed by the governor general for up to ten years.

A Supreme Court and magistrates' courts are responsible for the administration of justice. Every district capital has one magistrate's court, which is responsible for trying minor crimes, and Belize City has four. More serious crimes are tried by jury in the Supreme Court, and appeals can then be sent to the Court of Appeals. Justices of the Supreme Court are appointed by the governor general on advice from the prime minister and the leader

A policeman prepares to raise the Belize flag at a government office.

of the opposition, and are expected to be nonpolitical.

Belize is divided into six districts, which have district town boards made up of seven elected members (except for Belize City which has nine members) who have authority over local town affairs. Elections are held every three years. There are also elected village councils which help with local government.

NATIONAL DEFENSE

Until 1994 about 1,500 British troops, including about 300 air force personnel, were stationed in Belize. The defense of the country has now been passed to the Belize Defence Force, which was formed in 1978, from the existing Police Force and a Volunteer Guard. In 1992 the Belize Defence Force had an army of about 750 men, which included sea and air forces, and volunteers numbering about 500. Belize also has a Police Force of some 500 members, which sometimes works with the Defence Force in antinarcotics operations. The Defence Force also receives United States military assistance to combat drug traffickers who use Belize as a route to transport cocaine from South America to North America.

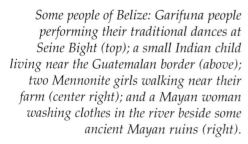

Some people of Belize: Garifuna people performing their traditional dances at Seine Bight (top); a small Indian child living near the Guatemalan border (above); two Mennonite girls walking near their farm (center right); and a Mayan woman washing clothes in the river beside some ancient Mayan ruins (right).

Chapter 5

PEOPLE OF BELIZE

One of the main reasons for the slow development of Belize is that the population has always been small. Even today there are only about 210,000 inhabitants, of whom about one-third live in Belize City.

The population is made up of several groups, each with its own history and culture. Few, if any, could claim direct descent from the original Maya inhabitants, and the majority have ancestors who arrived in Belize at different times over the last several hundred years. Yet despite their differences, the people of Belize have merged into an easygoing multi-ethnic society. Because there has been so much intermarriage, it is often difficult to tell to which group a person belongs, but surnames or the part of the country the person comes from may provide a clue.

Making up the population are the mestizos (sometimes called *ladinos*), the Creoles, the Maya, the Garifuna, who are also known as Black Caribs, and some recent immigrants. Mestizos are descendants of marriages between the native Indians and Europeans, mainly Spanish. Creoles are descended from marriages between African slaves and Europeans. The Garifuna have their origins in unions between African slaves and Carib Indians of the West Indies. In addition, immigrants have arrived in Belize from various parts of the world. They include a significant number of

A Creole girl collecting coconut shells from where they have been stored under her house

members of a religious sect, the Mennonites.

None of these groups is evenly spread through the country, rather each dominates in a particular region. For example, most of the people in Belize District are Creoles, while mestizos are predominant in Orange Walk District. More than half the population of rural Toledo is Mayan, while the Garifuna predominate in Dangriga.

THE CREOLES

African slaves arrived in Belize from about 1720 to the early 1800s. Unlike their compatriots sent to the West Indies, they were not forced into abject slavery on plantations. Instead, they worked in forests alongside European loggers, often in isolated, inhospitable regions. Loggers and slaves came to depend on each other, and sometimes slaves were able to buy their freedom.

Other blacks arrived who were not slaves. In 1817 when a West Indian Regiment of soldiers was disbanded, 500 men with land grants and some rations were transported to Belize, where they became free woodcutters. Others followed, adding some 700 people to a population of only 4,000. Survivors from a number of ships carrying men, women, and, in some cases, entire families, were also allowed to settle in Belize when their ships ran into difficulty offshore. There were three such instances in 1836 alone.

For many years, Creoles remained the largest group in the country, but the 1991 census showed that they now represent only about 30 percent of the population, while the mestizos account for 44 percent. Approximately two-thirds of Creoles live in the Belize District, while the population of Belize City is more than 50 percent Creole. For a first-time visitor, this can easily create the impression that the Creoles are still the most important group in the country. And in many ways they are, particularly in terms of culture and politics.

Creoles are more closely associated with British culture and traditions than other groups in Belize, and they have inherited many of the influential political jobs. The People's United Party has a strong Creole base, and the most important political figures in Belize are Creole. Preferring to live in the towns, Creoles dominate the civil service, but they also work as teachers, doctors, and lawyers. Many are in business and commerce. Others have remained in the countryside, often living alongside main highways and rivers. They have ceased to be loggers since the decline of the timber trade, and now earn a living as farmers or fishermen. Given an opportunity, they are also keen to learn new trades in industry and construction.

MESTIZOS

By far the majority of mestizos in Belize have arrived from other countries in Central America. The greatest influx occurred at the time of the War of the Races in Mexico's Yucatán. Thousands fled to safety across the border into northern Belize. Mainly farmers, the newcomers raised pigs, cultivated maize, and, most importantly, introduced sugarcane into Belize.

Waves of mestizos from Guatemala and El Salvador have been settling in Belize ever since, fleeing from the economic hardship, political instability, dictatorship, and terrorism that have dominated these countries for many years. Some of them take up seasonal work, cutting sugarcane or picking fruit. But there is concern that they are not well treated in these jobs. They receive the lowest pay, do the hardest jobs, and live in squalid conditions. Most cannot complain because they are illegal immigrants. Others have settled in small villages or cultivate clearings in the mountains to grow maize. In a United Nations-sponsored settlement, known as the Valley of Peace, near Belmopan, refugees have been given uncleared plots of forestland. Those who have ventured into urban areas sell small handicrafts and food snacks on the streets, and live in poor housing on the edges of the towns.

Historically, Belize has welcomed immigrants to supplement its own small population, and has offered health care and educational facilities. But there has been some resentment from Belizeans who at times feel their jobs are threatened. Also, an increase in crime has been associated with the refugees. With one out of every five persons a refugee, the government is also questioning whether it can continue to provide the necessary social services.

There is some concern, too, that Belize is becoming a mestizo country. While refugees have flooded in from the neighboring countries, large numbers of Creoles have been emigrating to the United States. They are attracted by the higher standard of living,

This Black Carib, or Garifuna, boy who lives near Stann Creek was eager to have his photograph taken.

better job prospects, North American culture, education, and other opportunities. In many ways, Belize is losing its black-based Creole identity.

GARIFUNA

Today it is often difficult to distinguish a Garifuna, or Black Carib, from a Creole. But their origins are quite different. At the time of the Spanish conquest, some Caribbean islands were occupied by a fierce, cannibalistic tribe known as the Red Caribs, who gradually overran the peaceful Arawak tribes in the region. But armed with only their bows and arrows, the Caribs proved no match for the Spaniards who had armor, horses, and gunpowder. By the seventeeth century, only small, scattered groups of Red Caribs remained on several tiny Caribbean islands.

In 1675, a ship carrying West African slaves was shipwrecked on one of those islands. The Black Carib people were born from the union between these two groups. By late in the eighteenth century, many Black Caribs were living on the West Indian island of St. Vincent, along with some runaway slaves from Barbados. Together, they plotted a rebellion against the British authorities. When the plot failed, they were deported to Roatán and other uninhabited islands in the Bay of Honduras.

From there it was only a short trip to the mainland to smuggle goods between British and Spanish Honduras (now the nation of Honduras), or to work as woodcutters. Traditionally their date of arrival in British Honduras is said to be November 19, 1802. That date is celebrated as Garifuna Settlement Day.

By the 1830s, many Garifuna were settled in the Stann Creek District where today about half the population is still Garifuna. In addition to Dangriga, Punta Negra and villages like Seine Bight and Hopkins are predominantly Garifuna. Elsewhere, in Belize City and Belmopan, there are communities of Garifuna, but overall they represent less than 7 percent of the population.

Traditionally the Garifuna worked as fishermen, using harpoons, hooks and line, and sometimes basketry fish traps made locally from reed. Today many more are turning to farming, once considered "women's work." But the Garifuna are quick to learn, and many are now employed in the civil service and as teachers.

There is a strong movement to retain the traditional culture of the Garifuna, which, because of its ancestry, is a rare ethnic mixture. A National Garifuna Council has been created. Garifunas still tend to marry within their own community, even though in their daily lives they mix freely with other Belizeans. There is resentment, though, between Garifuna and Creoles, largely because of their different cultural backgrounds.

THE MAYA

When the Europeans first arrived, Belize was inhabited by some scattered communities of Maya Indians. At different times both the English and Spanish raided these communities, and the

The workmen at the right (above left) are Mayans helping an anthropologist explore a 2,000-year-old irrigation ditch built by their ancestors. This Kekchi Mayan (right) carries wood much as his ancestors did. The Kekchi are the poorest ethnic group in Belize.

Maya who live in Belize today are largely descendants of groups that fled from Mexico and Guatemala in the last century. In the north are the Yucatec who arrived in the thousands as a result of the War of the Races, and settled between the Hondo and the New River. The other two groups are the Mopán and the Kekchi, who live in the districts of Cayo and Toledo. Both came from Guatemala, the Mopán to escape forced labor, heavy taxes, and military conscription, and the Kekchi fleeing from near-slavery on coffee plantations.

The Yucatec in the north have now merged with the local mestizo population to a greater extent than either the Mopán or the Kekchi, and many are rejecting their ancient traditions. Some now work in the forests collecting chicle. The lifestyle of the Mopán, and even more so, the Kekchi, has, however, remained much as before. They clear land by burning, and plant their *milpas,* or cleared plots, with corn and other crops for their own use, using the same primitive tools their ancestors did. They also hunt in the forests and fish in the rivers, selling any surplus in local markets. Some also now produce crops, such as rice and citrus fruits, to sell in town. While the men work on the milpas, the women take care of the homes and sometimes make small crafts to earn some extra money.

Living in a more remote area, the Kekchi are recognized as the poorest ethnic group in Belize. They have remained in touch with Kekchi villages in Guatemala, from whom they buy their cloth, as the Kekchi women in Belize no longer do their own weaving. The colorful striped or patterned cloth is used mainly for the traditional skirts and blouses which some of the women still wear.

The Maya make up about 11 percent of the Belizean people, their numbers having increased by continued immigration from Guatemala in the 1980s. Their villages are traditionally governed by an *alcalde* or headman, who is paid by the national government. In 1975 the Toledo Maya Cultural Council was established to protect Mayan culture and defend their rights. But there are difficulties. Some Maya prefer to ignore their own culture, hoping to integrate into the community as a whole. In addition, modern technology, radio and television, new roads, and land speculation all threaten what is left of traditional Mayan life and culture.

This Chinese immigrant to Belize runs a fish stand in the Belize City market.

IMMIGRANTS

Thousands of immigrants have crossed into Belize from parts of Central America and Mexico. Other groups have arrived from India, the Middle East, China, North America, and Europe.

In 1857, a massive, bloody uprising against the British resulted in the deportation of about a thousand soldiers from India to British Honduras. They were sent to work on the sugar plantations in the north, and today their descendants can be found there and in other parts of the country.

Only a few years later, the first Chinese immigrants arrived. They were imported by wealthy landowners to work as laborers, but their presence was resented by the mestizos, and many of the Chinese moved away. However, within recent years, more Chinese have arrived and are successfully running shops and restaurants in Belize City and elsewhere.

Other immigrants include descendants of North Americans who sought refuge in Belize during the American Civil War,

This strictly traditional Mennonite family looks like a family from one hundred years ago. They keep to themselves except when selling their goods to other Belizeans.

Lebanese merchants who have been highly successful in commerce and politics, and some Europeans.

Easily the most distinctive immigrants are the Mennonites, a religious sect that originated in northern Europe. In the face of persecution, and wishing to live by their own strict religious and moral code, they have been forced to move into countries where their way of life is tolerated. In 1959, some 3,000 Mennonites arrived in Belize and settled in the north around the River Hondo. It is essential to Mennonites that they remain a close-knit society and do not get involved with the affairs of the country in which they settle. They have their own form of government, which prohibits them from paying public taxes or being conscripted into the military. They marry only within their own community and educate their own children, who do not attend public schools. They do not use motor vehicles, which includes tractors and other farm equipment, and they travel about in horse-drawn buggies.

The Mennonites are very competent and successful farmers. This was proved soon after their arrival in Belize when their economic production of eggs cut the market price by half. Today they produce about 80 percent of the country's food, selling through a warehouse in Belize City and on a door-to-door basis. They are responsible for making chicken the national dish. About 8,000 Mennonites live in Belize, owning large areas of land, though not all is yet cultivated. They have created well-ordered rural communities with European-style houses and small gardens.

Some division is beginning to occur among the Mennonites. There are six main communities in the north and northwest, and, of these, the two at Blue Creek and Spanish Lookout are adopting a more progressive lifestyle. Many no longer wear the traditional dress. They have telephones, drive their own trucks, and use modern farm machinery. Also, they have founded some evangelical churches that hope to attract new members. This is not in the tradition of the Mennonites, who do not normally preach their creed outside their community. It is also in striking contrast to their usual isolation. Visitors are viewed from behind closed windows, and while Mennonites will respectfully return a greeting of "Good morning" or "Good day," they seldom are the first to offer it.

LANGUAGES

English is the official language of Belize. Its early, rather old-fashioned form is still used in business and politics. But the

These Belizean children, from several different ethnic groups, are learning about their homeland in English.

English spoken among Creoles is very different from the language used in the United States or Britain. It is a mixture of English with local Creole words and foreign expressions, spoken with a sing-song lilt that many visitors find difficult to understand. Spanish is the natural language of the mestizos and is also understood by many of the Maya. As the number of mestizos increases, Spanish is becoming more widely used. There is also a form of Creole Spanish.

The minority groups in Belize have all retained their own languages, though most also have a knowledge of English or Spanish. The Garifuna are keen to preserve their language and would like to introduce it into the school system. Among the Maya, those in the north tend to speak Spanish rather than their native tongue, but the other two groups still use the Mayan language, though with different dialects. The Mennonites speak among themselves in their traditional German-Dutch dialect.

Many people in Belize speak more than one language, but the language most widely spoken in any one area relates to the most numerous group of people there. So in the Belize District and Belize City, English or Creole English is the usual language, while in the Corozal or Orange Walk districts, Spanish predominates.

Chapter 6

LIFE AND WORK
IN BELIZE

If the population of Belize were spread evenly over the country, there would be about 23 persons per 1 square mile (2.6 square kilometers). But the distribution is uneven, and over half the population lives in just seven towns. By far the majority—about 50,000—are in Belize City.

The towns have continued to increase in size for several reasons. Many people have moved from the countryside looking for a better way of life. Towns have medical and educational facilities not found in rural areas. Also, with better health, the birth rate has improved. Immigrants from other Central American countries have helped swell the numbers, particularly in the western towns of San Ignacio and Benque Viejo. The most rapid urban growth has been in the northern towns of Corozal and Orange Walk, where the population increased threefold during the twenty years between 1960 and 1980.

Finding work in the towns is not easy, and it is particularly difficult for new arrivals. Few have any skills to offer and must turn their hand to whatever they can. They may work as cleaners, gardeners, or occasionally as domestic servants. If lucky enough to own or have use of a car, they can become taxi drivers, but many make their way to the streets where they sell food snacks or small handicrafts. With the increasing number of mestizos from Central America, there has been a noticeable increase in the sidewalk stalls selling such Spanish-style foods as tortillas and tacos.

The majority of town workers are employed in service industries, including banking, insurance and financial institutions, hotel and restaurant industries, and tourism. Tourism, in particular, recently has offered more opportunities for employment. Greater numbers of tourists are visiting Belize than ever before, and this has meant more work for people in the construction business, building new hotels and facilities, and for people involved in the transport industry. Other skilled and semiskilled workers are employed in manufacturing industries, and in factories producing processed foods and drinks, textiles, and clothing. Most professional people, such as doctors, lawyers, and teachers, are also based in the towns.

Most people living outside the towns work on the land. For some communities like the Maya, this means milpa farming and, usually, producing only enough food for their own use. Others, however, work on farms using modern machinery to grow a variety of crops for sale. Belizeans produce enough corn, beans, and, until recently, rice, that they do not need to import these foods. Another form of farming is on large estates or plantations usually owned by wealthy landlords or multinational companies, and whose produce is almost entirely exported.

Both large and small farmers are involved in growing and cutting sugarcane, which they sell to factories for processing into sugar, the country's main export. Most of the sugarcane is grown in the north, and people have moved from all parts of the country to find work in the cane fields and processing plants.

Belize is a land of contrasts (clockwise from top): The town of Dangriga, or Stann Creek, changes quickly from urban to rural when seen from the air. San Ignacio in the western part of the country can be reached by this suspension bridge. Orange Walk, in the north, has a major sugar refinery. Not far away, at San Felipe, people lived in thatched huts.

The downtown area (left) and some typical residences (right) in Belize City, the largest city in Belize

The number of women working has steadily increased, with most employed in the service industries and particularly in the textile factories. Men make up most of the workforce in agriculture and industry. Overall, though, the rate of unemployment remains high, at around 15 percent. The number would be much higher if it also included part-time workers, or those people employed only seasonally, such as the sugarcane cutters.

BELIZE CITY

The city where Belize began and which was its capital through most of its history was built on a point of land barely 3 miles (4.8 kilometers) wide. It is about 5 miles (8 kilometers) from the mouth of the Belize River and just a few inches above sea level. Swampy ground and numerous canals spread in every direction. The only raised parts were natural mud banks or levees of silt, or alluvium, carried from the interior by the river and deposited where the current slowed.

The first settlers chose the northern bank of a river branch they knew as Haulover Creek as the place to build log houses and straw huts for their slaves. It was not until the nineteenth century that the city began to grow. The first steps were taken when the south bank of the river was protected by wooden piles and a bridge was built across the creek. The canal above the bridge was straightened and other canals were dug through parts of the town to carry the waters away. The log huts were gradually replaced by well-built wooden houses and, later, brick and concrete set on foundations or stilts to raise them above the level of any potential flooding. They were not high enough, however, to escape the huge waves blown in from the sea by the hurricane of September 10, 1931, and the city was inundated to a depth of 15 feet (4.5 meters).

After that great hurricane, much of the city had to be rebuilt. Even St. John's, the cathedral constructed from bricks brought from England, was damaged, with its roof and windows blown away. St. John's, built in 1812, is the oldest Anglican church in Central America.

Other landmarks date from the same time. Fort George was a small fort erected on a swampy island at the mouth of the river's estuary in 1803. At one time the island was connected to the main-land by a small bridge, but in 1922 a contract to develop the land was awarded to an American company. Over the next two years the tiny canal between the island and the mainland was filled and a concrete wall was erected around the island. This work made the area, known as Fort George, one of the most desirable residential places in Belize city. Grand wooden mansions set between palms and bougainvillea stand on one side of a small park and, on the other, overlooking the sea is the Fort George lighthouse and the tomb of Baron Bliss.

Perhaps the city's most illustrious benefactor, Baron Bliss,

The Supreme Court building in Belize City (left) was previously the colonial courthouse. The monument to Baron Bliss (right) acknowledges the great help this benefactor gave to Belize.

otherwise known as Henry Edward Ernest Bliss, 4th Baron of the Kingdom of Portugal, was born in Buckinghamshire County in England. In 1926 Baron Bliss spent many months in Belize Harbor on his yacht, *Sea King*, but was too ill with stomach problems to go ashore. He was treated so well by the concerned people of Belize that he set aside a fortune of two million dollars in trust to benefit the country. The interest earned by his bequest has since financed many public works including markets, a health center, public buildings, a road, and the Baron Bliss Institute, as well as the purchase of the land where the new capital, Belmopan, is built.

The largest area of the city is south of Haulover Creek. Near the sea and behind a low protecting wall stands the Supreme

Haulover Creek is the center of much activity in Belize City. A manually controlled swing bridge (left) is opened every day. An open market (right) serves people both on land and on boats.

Court building built of fine wood and surmounted by a wooden clock tower. This is actually the third court building on the site. One of the earlier courthouses was destroyed by fire.

Other buildings here include the banks and a long-established general store. Eight blocks away and set in small grounds facing the sea stands Government House. Behind these substantial buildings there are many streets of poorer housing, some of it next to narrow canals. Often the paint is flaking from many seasons of tropical heat and rain that have also left wood rotting and shutters hanging loose. At one time, the only fresh water came from rain collected in large vats below the roofs, but since the late 1940s water has been piped to the city from a source 9 miles (14.5 kilometers) away, near the airport.

For over half a century one of the most notable daily events in Belize City has been the opening of the iron "swing bridge" that crosses Haulover Creek near its mouth. The bridge is balanced carefully on a pivot so the entire roadway can be turned through 90 degrees to allow small vessels to enter the safety of the creek. Early every morning the road traffic is stopped by the bridge-

Government office buildings in the new capital city of Belmopan

master while a team of men insert a handle in a "key hole" beside the road. As they turn the handle, it connects with a mechanism below and the bridge slowly swings open. This historic bridge has been under threat of closure for some years, but so far only the new Belcan Bridge 1 mile (1.6 kilometers) upriver has been built, to give better access to the Northern and Western Highways.

BELMOPAN

The name of the new capital city comes from *Beli*ze and the Maya tribe, the *Mopán*. Hurricane Hattie gave the impetus for the long-considered plan to move the capital inland. In 1965 the site was cleared in dry forest about 50 miles (80 kilometers) from Belize City and a few miles south of the Western Highway. Once the site was ready, the first buildings of a modern city were constructed following a design from a firm of London architects. Contrasting strongly with other buildings in Belize, the style of Belmopan contains elements of the present century combined with some Mayan design influence.

Lines of shallow steps rise between lawns to the National Assembly building where the Belize flag is raised each day. Low, spacious, and well-lighted government offices stand on two sides of the grounds, where people can walk among modern sculptures. Around this focal area, the Bank of Belize, the Magistrate's Court, Police Headquarters, and the bus station have been built. The residential area, churches, a hospital, and schools are located away from the center. The planning leaves plenty of room for expansion, and population projections suggest that the capital could have as many as 30,000 inhabitants. But by the mid-1990s, almost thirty years after it was started, less than 5,000 people live in Belmopan, a reflection on the Belizean preference for remaining near the center of things, Belize City.

EDUCATION

The standard of education in Belize is good compared with other countries in Central America, and the rate of literacy is high, with officially about 90 percent of the people able to read or write. The real rate may be rather lower as some people can write little more than their names and simple sentences.

The first school was founded in 1816 by the Church of England, beginning a tradition by which most schools are now run by the churches. The Roman Catholic Church, Anglicans, and Methodists administer most of the primary schools, with the Roman Catholic Church alone responsible for about 60 percent of all the schools in Belize.

The system was endorsed by the British colonial administration, and it was not until the 1950s and the beginning of the nationalist

A teacher working with a primary student (left),
and another teacher working with three women who
are learning to become teachers themselves (above)

movement that politicians began to query the government's lack of role in education. But rather than creating a state educational system, the government opted to subsidize the church-run schools. It pays most of the teachers' salaries and runs about 10 percent of the primary schools. Government spending on education averages from 15 to 20 percent of Belize's national budget, which is much more than is spent on any other single item.

By law all children should attend primary school for eight years, between the ages of 5 and 14. Primary school is free and an average class is about 25 students to each teacher. Secondary education, beginning at the age of 12, lasts four or five years. Schooling follows the British system, with the principal subjects being English, mathematics, history, and geography. Examinations must be passed before students can move into a higher grade. But many children do not complete their education, some because they are needed by their families to help at home and on the land, others because there is no school nearby. It has been calculated that only just over half of the children registered for primary school complete the required eight years. A much smaller number complete secondary school, and only a tiny minority go on to higher education. Another problem is the differing standards between rural and town schools. The rural schools are much less well-equipped and generally have less qualified teachers.

For those students able to move into higher education, there are opportunities to study technical, vocational, and teacher-training courses. The University College of Belize was established in 1986, and there is also a branch of the University of the West Indies in Belize. Students, teachers, and administrators have also been able to study in the United States as part of aid programs, while volunteers from Britain and the Peace Corps from the United States have worked in schools in Belize.

HEALTH AND SOCIAL WELFARE

Compared with many developing countries, the standard of health and welfare in Belize is high. This is largely due to the efforts of the government to provide more medical facilities and to improve some of the basic conditions that lead to good health. In addition, Belize has received considerable help from international nongovernment organizations. They have worked with the government to improve living conditions, water, and sewage facilities and to educate people into preparing better-balanced and more nutritious meals.

For many years, tropical diseases such as yellow fever and smallpox were a major cause of death, but these have been stopped. Malaria, especially in the south, is still one of the main causes of people needing hospital treatment.

There are hospitals in all the major towns, though most surgeons are based in Belize City, which has the most modern facilities. The countryside is served by rural and mobile clinics. However, many rural people live too far from the clinics to easily get medical help. About a quarter of the population is still without access to any health facilities. People in some remote communities practice traditional medicine, using plants from the forest and their own remedies. The government is trying to ease the problem by providing health-care training to selected people from the villages. But even in the towns, there is a shortage of nurses. Most of them are trained in the local Belize College of Nursing, but they are poorly paid and many seek employment in Mexico or the United States.

Yet, despite the problems, people are in better health, living longer than previously. Fewer babies die at birth, and today an estimated 45 percent of the population is under 14 years old. But it is not health care alone that has brought this about. Equally important is good, clean water. Almost everyone living in the towns now has access to a supply, and about two-thirds of them have water piped into their homes. People in the rural areas fare less well, with only about half able to get good drinking water.

A good health program also encourages people to eat more nutritious foods, and while this has been partially successful, there is concern that almost a fifth of children between the ages of one and four are considered to be suffering from malnutrition. This high percentage is partly due to the influx of refugees from other Central American countries.

Two very different, but beautiful, houses in Belize. The one on the left is out in the jungle and lacks all amenities except the setting. The one on the right was built in colonial days and now serves as a restaurant and inn.

HOUSING

Most of the houses in Belize are built of wood, clapboard style, with corrugated iron roofs. They have many windows, or sometimes just shutters that remain open all day in normal weather but can be closed to give protection in strong winds. Many homes are built on wooden or concrete stilts to avoid possible floods and to make the upper rooms more airy. The lower rooms are used only for kitchens or storage. Almost everyone has a balcony, which can be used to hang out washing but is also somewhere to sit in warm evenings. Because of the history of damaging hurricanes in coastal towns, some homes now have a brick base and others are of cement block.

A few rather grand colonial-style mansions have survived, with fine stairways leading to the upper front door and decorative ironwork and wooden balconies on most levels. But apart from these and the recent housing developments in the cays, much of

This typical house outside a central city (left) has a tin roof. Most houses out in the countryside have thatched roofs (right). A new building being thatched with palm fronds is shown here.

the housing in towns appears run-down, despite efforts by the owners to paint their homes in a variety of colors. An average home may have two or three rooms, shared by possibly several generations of one family. The accommodation is basic with mostly just essential furniture, but most have sanitation facilities and electricity.

Outside the towns, homes are also made of wood, but in very rural areas, roofing is of coconut or cohune palm thatch. Some homes are built of flattened metal strips or adobe mud brick. In the countryside, many homes are brightened by the profusion of colorful tropical trees and plants surrounding the house.

FOOD

The variety of dishes in Belize reflects the tastes and customs of the mixed population, and traditionally includes Creole, Mexican, Chinese, and European. Fast-foods of the kind served in the United States are relatively new. The most typical "national dish"

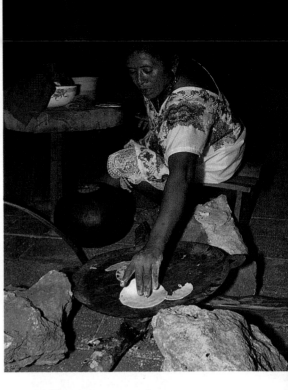

A Mayan woman making tortillas in her hut near the Yucatán border

is chicken with rice, beans, or plantains (a greenish, starchy vegetable), which is eaten in most homes and restaurants.

Among the Maya and the mestizos, corn (maize) and beans have remained the staple foods, in much the same way as they have in Mexico and the rest of Central America. Maize is used to make tortillas, which can be filled 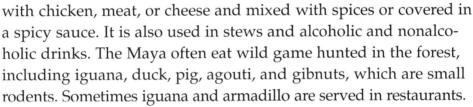 with chicken, meat, or cheese and mixed with spices or covered in a spicy sauce. It is also used in stews and alcoholic and nonalcoholic drinks. The Maya often eat wild game hunted in the forest, including iguana, duck, pig, agouti, and gibnuts, which are small rodents. Sometimes iguana and armadillo are served in restaurants.

The most exciting Belizean food is the local fresh fish. In addition to lobster, conch, and shrimp, there are red snapper, sea bass, halibut, barracuda, and many others, all cooked in a variety of ways. Conch, for example, is used to make *ceviche,* which is raw fish marinaded in lime juice, with onions, peppers, and spices and eaten with sweet potatoes. A "boil-up" is a seafood stew seasoned with onions and peppers. A typical Garifuna dish is seafood gumbo, which combines conch, lobster, shrimp, and other fish with vegetables cooked in coconut milk, herbs, and grated plantains, usually served with rice. Or there is *tapow,* in which sliced plantains are simmered in coconut milk with fish, herbs, and seasonings.

The baptism of a Mayan young person is being held in the open sea (left). St. John's Cathedral (above) is the oldest Anglican church in Central America. It was built of bricks brought across the sea from England.

RELIGION

The people of Belize can practice whatever religion they choose. Most are Roman Catholic, but their number has been decreasing in recent years. In Central and South America, Catholicism was introduced by priests who accompanied the Spanish soldiers and settlers. But this did not happen in Belize where the British loggers, if anything, would have belonged to the Protestant Church. The Roman Catholic Church in Belize is strong today as a result of the arrival of mestizos and others from Mexico and Central America, and because of the work of American Jesuit priests. Jesuits now administer five of the country's twelve parishes, and also maintain St. John's College, the prestigious secondary school in Belize City, which George Price and many

These children attend a school run by an evangelical church in the small town of Hattieville.

other leading Belizeans attended. Being responsible for some 60 percent of the schools in Belize has also meant that the Roman Catholic Church has exerted considerable influence in education.

Other churches in Belize include the Anglicans (Church of England) and the Methodists, but the Anglicans, like the Roman Catholics, are losing members to new evangelical sects from the United States. These include the Assemblies of God, Baptists, Seventh Day Adventists, Jehovah's Witnesses, and the Mormons. Most do not limit their work to Sunday services and preaching but have introduced social service projects including schools, education through the media, and Bible studies. Some people are concerned that these projects, which are funded and sponsored by the North American evangelical churches, are basically changing the nature of Belizean society. Concern has also been expressed that such missionary work among the Maya is contributing to the breakdown of their traditional culture.

TRANSPORTATION

All the time timber was floated down rivers to the coastal ports, nobody in Belize bothered with any other kind of transport. Until the 1930s, there was hardly a road anywhere in the country, and Belize City was connected to other towns on the coast only by boat. But with the development of the sugar industry, roads became a necessity to transport the cane to the factories and then to the ports. To begin with, few of the roads were paved. Instead, they were dirt tracks full of potholes best traveled by horse and cart or a very rugged vehicle. Even as late as the 1950s, there were only 500 automobiles in the entire country.

The first main road to be built was the Northern Highway, which runs from Belize City to the Mexican border, where a bridge across the River Hondo connects with the Mexican town of Chetumal. This was followed by the Western Highway, completed in 1948, which crosses the country from Belize City to Benque Viejo on the Guatemalan border. The first part of this road is the main highway between Belize City and Belmopan and is the best maintained road in Belize. Belmopan is near the junction of the Western Highway and the narrow, 52-mile (84-kilometer) Hummingbird Highway, which runs southeast through beautiful jungle scenery and orange and grapefruit groves, to Dangriga. The Southern Highway between Dangriga and Punta Gorda is the only other major route.

There is now a total of 882 miles (1419 kilometers) of all-weather roads in Belize, and 405 miles (651 kilometers) of cart roads and bush trails. Improvements to the Hummingbird Highway have been financed by the European Community. But

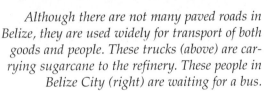

Although there are not many paved roads in Belize, they are used widely for transport of both goods and people. These trucks (above) are carrying sugarcane to the refinery. These people in Belize City (right) are waiting for a bus.

except for the major highways, the roads are rough and potholed, and when it rains, only a four-wheel vehicle can cope with the deep, muddy ruts.

Belizeans drive on the right side of the road, as in the United States. There is a very high rate of traffic accidents, especially in Belize City. Even so, most people have little choice but to travel around the country on public buses, which are frequent and fairly reliable. Perhaps the best known is the Batty Bus Service. There are now no railroads in Belize, and air services are expensive.

Belize does not have a national airline but is dependent on foreign airlines to bring visitors from the United States, Mexico, and other Central American countries. Travelers from other parts of the world generally fly first to the United States or Mexico for a connection to Belize City. Airlines arrive at the recently improved

This ferry (above) carries people and goods of all kinds across the Mopán River. Although sailboats in Belizean waters are primarily for recreation, this one (right) is carrying cargo in a traditional fashion.

Philip Goldson International Airport 10 miles (16 kilometers) from Belize City. Within Belize, Maya Airways flies daily to each main town, and several of the cays and smaller towns have airstrips.

River transport is still used in the interior, while regular ferries and boats carry passengers around the cays. There is a deepwater port at Belize City and a second port at Commerce Bight, near Dangriga. Among recent projects designed to help boost the economy is a new deepwater port at Big Creek.

COMMUNICATION

There are no daily newspapers in Belize, but there are six weekly publications whose circulation seldom reaches outside

Belize City. International news items are very limited, but the papers report on local issues and sport. Two of the weeklies are strongly political: the *People's Pulse*, which reflects the views of the UDP, and the *Belize Times*, which supports the PUP. The most independent paper is the *Amandala*, while business items are high on the agenda of the *Reporter. Amandala* has the largest circulation, at about 8,000, followed by the *Reporter* with around 6,500. A small weekly, the *San Pedro Sun*, is published in San Pedro. Although the newspapers are predominantly in English, more articles are appearing in Spanish, in an attempt to attract a wider audience.

Radio broadcasts are in English and Spanish, and radio is the most influential form of media as programs are received widely throughout the country. In 1990 over 100,000 radio receivers were in use. Belize Radio One is the main channel, and it includes in its schedules programs of both general interest and some aimed specifically at ethnic and other small groups. For example, programs include the "Garifuna Half Hour," the "Ketchi Show," and the "Mopán Maya Show." A new, private station, Radio KREM, which features local music, is also proving very popular.

Television, which is relatively new to Belize, has four main channels. Because of lack of money, training, and resources, few programs, other than talk shows and some documentaries, are made locally. The majority of programs come from the United States, pirated from satellite transmissions. Television and radio are the responsibility of the Broadcasting Corporation of Belize (BCB), an independent organization, free of government control.

Belize has an efficient telephone service, and it is possible to dial direct to any country in the world. Telephone service is cheaper than from the neighboring Central American countries.

Uncovered Mayan artifacts show the ancient arts of Belize, such as these carved details on El Castillo at Xunantunich (above) and this stone stela, or carved pillar, found at Lamanai (below), which fascinates tourists.

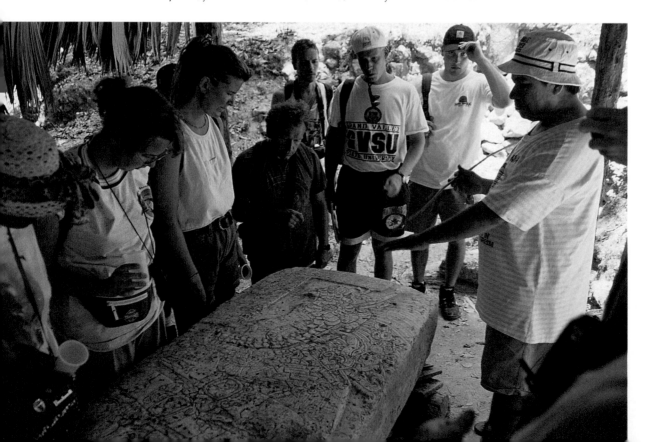

Chapter 7

CULTURE
AND THE ARTS

THE MAYA

There are many sites associated with the old Mayan civilization dotted around Belize that bear witness to the artistic, cultural, and engineering skills of these pre-Columbian people. Other sites still lie undetected or partly hidden within the forests, and new discoveries are being made every year.

The site most extensively excavated is Altún Ha, about 30 miles (48.3 kilometers) north of Belize City. Much of it is still covered by trees, but there is enough evidence to show that it was both a major religious center and a trading center. Probably built about 1,500 to 2,000 years ago, Altún Ha has two main plazas surrounded by structures that were palaces and temples. Among these, overlooking one plaza and some 60 feet (18.2 meters) high is the Temple of the Sun God. Close to the other plaza is a reservoir, which provided water for the ancient inhabitants. Known as Rockstone Pond, the name translates into Mayan as Altún Ha. The construction of the reservoir is a good example of the skill of Mayan engineers, as it involved diverting a jungle stream, and then building a large pit which they plastered with limestone

Chac, the rain god, is a frequent symbol in ancient Mayan stonework.

cement, before re-diverting the stream again to fill the pit.

Within tombs at Altún Ha archeologists have discovered many artifacts, including more than 300 jade pieces, jewelry such as earrings and rings, and some green obsidian blades. But the most exciting find was in the Temple of the Green Tomb. Hidden deep at the top of this pyramid were the remains of an important person, covered with jade, pearls, and beads. Beside the body was a solid jade head now known as Kinich Ahau, the Sun God. Weighing some 9.5 pounds (4.3 kilograms), it is the largest piece of carved jade ever found.

Another site not far from Altún Ha is *Lamanai,* meaning "submerged crocodile," which is one of the largest ceremonial centers in Belize. The name derives from some large masks that archeologists discovered, depicting a ruler wearing a crocodile headdress. Jade jewelry and masks have also been found, as well as pottery dating back to 100 B.C.

Xunantunich, near San Ignacio and close to the Guatemalan border, is perhaps the most beautiful site in Belize. It is a small excavation, but its spectacular main temple, El Castillo, is one of the highest in Belize. From the top there is a magnificent view across the jungle of Guatemala's Petén, and the hilly Cayo District of Belize. Here many stelae and *friezes* (carved-stone wall panels) covered in intricately carved glyphs have been found.

The Mayan site at Caracol is only now being excavated. No one yet knows just how big it will prove to be. This structure is the Canaa, *or "sky palace."*

Possibly the largest site in Belize, but one which has yet to reveal its secrets, is Caracol, isolated deep in the jungle south of San Ignacio. Excavations have revealed that its main pyramid is, at 136 feet (41.4 meters), slightly higher than the one at Xunantunich, and is perhaps the largest of all the structures in Belize. There are reservoirs, agricultural terraces, plazas, temples, causeways, and numerous glyphs and carvings. The name *Caracol* means "snail," from the many shells found on the site.

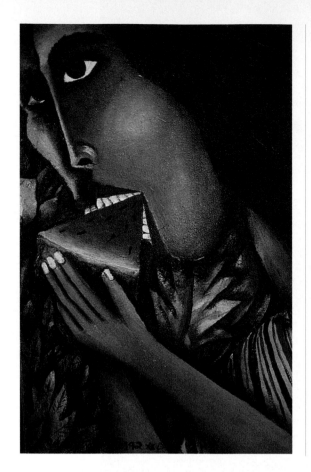

A recent painting by Belizean artist Nelson Young is on display in a museum in Santo Domingo.

CULTURE AND THE ARTS

Cultural traditions in Belize are of very mixed origins and relate to the different ethnic groups in the country. There has been little opportunity for a national culture to emerge, although since independence some artists, poets, and writers, including novelist Zee Edgell, have had work published and shown.

Music and dance are the most popular form of artistic expression and incorporate the rhythms and beat of Africa and the Caribbean, together with modern pop music from Europe and the United States. From the Caribbean comes reggae, soka—a more raucous form of reggae—steel drums, and, at festival time, the loud and carefree "jump up" dance.

In contrast, Creole folk songs can be melodious, with sad and happy themes sung in the Creole patois. Very traditional are "break-downs" or "brukdowns," which began in the logging camps in the 1800s. They were originally songs improvised on the spot to tell a story or to make fun of an important person. Some years ago they were usually accompanied by a steel band, but today guitars, banjos, and harmonicas are also played. Another local instrument is the marimba, a form of wooden xylophone,

A farmer in the country near Belmopan serenades passersby with an old guitar (left). Passersby in Belize City may be entertained by a marimba band (right).

while the Kekchi Maya use violins, harps, and guitars, all stringed instruments introduced by the Spaniards.

There has recently been a revival of Garifuna *punta* music, which traditionally the women sang to each other in a form of "call and response." Modernized, it has become punta rock and has been successfully recorded for the international market.

Some ethnic dances that have survived among the Kekchi Maya are usually performed at the time of the fiesta of San Luis, which takes place in San Antonio village in the Toledo District in September.

The two best-known dances are the Tiger Dance and the Holy Deer Dance. Performed in the village square, the Tiger Dance is a comic confrontation between the tiger, as a clown, and men hunters dressed in red. The Deer Dance is more solemn and lasts several days, during which the deer disappears into the forest. The drama unfolds as "dogs" and hunters dressed in black pursue the deer, who is eventually found. Chased back to the village, the frightened deer is ceremoniously killed by the hunters.

The clear waters around the cays attract snorkelers and other people who like water sports.

LEISURE

Apart from festivals connected with the religious calendar, such as Christmas and Easter, Belizeans celebrate a number of national holidays. These include Baron Bliss Day, when after a formal ceremony at his tomb near the lighthouse, a day of fishing and sailing follows, as he requested in his will. St. George's Cay Day commemorates the defeat of the Spaniards on September 10, 1798, and everyone takes to the streets for a week-long carnival. Just eleven days later, is National Independence Day, when the streets are again filled with people enjoying music and dance.

Dangriga town is the setting for Garifuna Settlement Day, which relives the arrival of the first Garifuna in Belize. It takes the form of a pageant when two dugout canoes paddle upriver from the open sea. Onboard are a few simple provisions such as the original Garifuna might have carried. Once ashore, the boat-party joins in a colorful procession, backed by the sound of drums, to the Catholic Church, to give thanks. Dancing and singing continue long into the night.

Organized sport in Belize is limited largely to clubs, which only a small number of people can afford. But with the barrier reef and some beautiful beaches, there is every opportunity to indulge in water sports. Swimming, scuba diving, snorkeling, boating, and fishing are all very popular, and many people in Belize like to spend their leisure time and holidays in and on the water.

Chapter 8

THE ECONOMY
AND THE WORLD

From the 1600s to the 1960s, timber was the mainstay of the Belizean economy. First the settlers cut and exported logwood, then they moved on to mahogany and other hardwoods which, especially during the eighteenth and nineteenth centuries, were in great demand for fine furniture. In time there were few mahogany trees left within easy reach of the rivers, and loggers found it difficult to penetrate the forest to find more. There were no roads, because loggers had always depended on the rivers to transport the logs. Some loggers turned to chicle-gathering, spending their days tapping the sapodilla trees for the sap used in the chewing-gum industry.

In the 1950s, timber represented about 75 percent of the value of all exports, and the industry employed some 3,000 workers. However, less than twenty years later the number of workers had declined dramatically to 1,000, and, by the 1990s, forestry represented less than 3 percent of export income. Even so, with almost half the country covered in forest, timber could still be commercially viable, provided it is supported by reforestation and conservation programs.

Agriculture was not developed in Belize until late in the last century. Because of the success of the timber industry, there was no need to introduce a plantation economy using hundreds of slaves to grow sugar or bananas as many Caribbean islands had done. Also, the Spanish authorities consistently did not allow the loggers to own land. Any farming was limited to families growing only enough food to feed themselves.

Today Belize's most important commercial crop is sugar. Although it was grown in the seventeenth century, serious cultivation did not begin until the arrival of the mestizos from Mexico during the War of the Races. Bananas were introduced in the 1880s, and the first citrus fruit, grapefruit, was planted in 1913.

When Belize became independent in 1981, the economy was in bad shape and had to be bailed out by the International Monetary Fund. It agreed to a loan on condition that the government introduce a number of strict measures, including raising taxes. By the mid-1980s, the world economic scene had improved greatly and Belize's agricultural produce were selling well. During the late 1980s and early 1990s, the Belize economy experienced an average annual growth rate of about 9 percent, which was much higher than most of the rest of the Caribbean and Central American economies.

There has also been increased private and public investment in Belize since its cays and beaches have been discovered as tourist destinations by the world. Another factor that contributes to the economy, and provides an important source of income, are the substantial funds sent back to Belize by Belizeans working in the United States. As much as a quarter of all Belize's foreign exchange comes from this source.

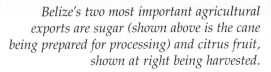

Belize's two most important agricultural exports are sugar (shown above is the cane being prepared for processing) and citrus fruit, shown at right being harvested.

AGRICULTURE

About half the working population of Belize is employed in agriculture, though only 10 to 15 percent of the potentially good arable land is cultivated. Sugar is by far the most successful crop, with exports accounting for about a third of export income, which is just less than the combined total of citrus fruits and bananas. Most of the sugar is grown in the northern districts of Corozal and Orange Walk, where some 5,000 sugarcane farmers cultivate almost 60,000 acres (24,000 hectares). There are large and small independent sugarcane farmers, although only in recent years have the small farmers been allowed to own land. During the harvesting season, the farmers have to rely on seasonal workers from El Salvador and Guatemala to cut the cane.

By the 1960s, a giant British Company, Tate & Lyle, was operating two factories where cane supplied by the farmers was processed into sugar and molasses, which is used in the production of ethanol,

Many farmers and fishermen contribute to the Belizean economy in a small way.
This farmer (left) is processing coconuts into oil. These fishermen hauling nets at
Dangriga (right) will sell their catch.

a fuel alcohol used in cars as an alternative to gasoline. Sugar is
also used for the local rum. In the 1970s there was a boom in the
production of sugar and molasses, but the market slumped in the
early 1980s. In 1985 Tate & Lyle sold most of their interest in the
factories to a local company, the Belize Sugar Industries.

The second most important agricultural product is citrus fruits,
particularly grapefruit and oranges. Citrus fruits are grown mainly
in the Stann Creek District, where there are two processing plants
that turn the fruits into concentrated juice for export. The first
commercial production of citrus fruits dates back to the 1920s, but
it was not until 1984 that the industry took off. In that year, the
United States removed taxes from citrus fruits grown in the
Caribbean. Shortly afterward, Belize's sales received a further
boost when the fruit industry in Florida and Texas was damaged
by severe frost. In ten years—from 1980 to 1990—the export value
of citrus fruits trebled, and in 1992 it was twice that of 1991. The

40,000 acres (16,200 hectares) of land given over to citrus cultivation is increasing daily as small farmers revamp their fields to start growing oranges and grapefruit.

For most of this century, attempts to create a profitable banana industry have been plagued by disease of the plants and devastation caused by hurricanes. The plantations are based in the Stann Creek and Toledo districts. In 1971 trees resistant to disease were introduced, and by the end of the 1980s banana exports had increased significantly. But in exporting bananas, Belize is in competition with many other Central American countries whose yields per acre are greater. Other produce grown for export includes winter vegetables, papayas, mangoes, and cocoa.

FISHING

Until thirty years ago, the fishing industry in Belize supplied only the local market. Then, in the 1960s, fishermen organized themselves into cooperatives, in which, working together, they could collectively sell their catch. Fishing contributes significantly to the economy. Lobster, conch, and shrimp are the main fish caught for export, and between 1991 and 1992, the export of shrimp doubled.

However, the cooperatives are faced with the problem of overfishing in Belizean waters. Catches of lobster and conch declined in the 1980s, and there is a fear that the same may happen to shrimp if it is not carefully farmed, with restrictions on the size of catch taken. Apart from the export market, there is also the local tourist industry, to whom fishermen sell illegal catches. Lobster and shrimp are among the most popular dishes in restaurants, and

Furniture manufactured in the Mennonite community being sold in Belize City

these seafoods need to be available, fresh, all year round.

INDUSTRY

Industry, not well advanced in Belize, employs only 15 percent of the population. There are a small number of factories making goods mainly for the local market, such as beer, soft drinks, cigarettes, furniture, and building materials. Others are connected with the agricultural industry and process sugar, citrus fruit concentrate, and feed for animals. The most recent venture into manufacturing is in making clothing for the American market. There are several foreign-owned factories, and clothing now represents a respectable percentage of the export market. Belizeans themselves can make a short trip to the Mexican border where there is a plentiful supply of relatively cheap goods.

The workforce in Belize is small and largely unskilled, yet, compared with its Central American neighbors, the workers are well paid. However, other Central American countries can offer lower-priced industrial goods because they have greater and cheaper supplies of energy. Belize has to import all its petroleum,

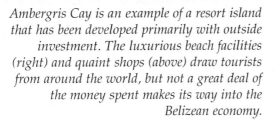

Ambergris Cay is an example of a resort island that has been developed primarily with outside investment. The luxurious beach facilities (right) and quaint shops (above) draw tourists from around the world, but not a great deal of the money spent makes its way into the Belizean economy.

although exploration for oil has been taking place in the northwest for some years. There is also the possibility of oil and gas deposits offshore. Electricity is expensive, though a new hydroelectric plant on the Macal River should reduce its cost.

Lack of a good transport network across the country also limits industrial growth. Considerable strides are being made in improving or building new roads, ports, and airports, and presently the construction business is the country's fastest-growing industry.

TOURISM

The construction industry has been given a big boost by the development of tourism, which, besides roads and good transport,

Left: For those who don't want to snorkel, glass-bottomed boats can show tourists the life in the warm, shallow sea around Belize.
Right: Many beaches, such as this one at Placentia, have not yet been developed and provide places for inexpensive beach houses.

needs hotels. Between 1974 and 1994, more than 200 hotels were built. In 1980 some 64,000 tourists visited Belize. By 1992 that figure had risen to 247,346, almost half from the United States.

Belize has a great deal to offer the tourist. The main attraction is the spectacular barrier reef and the cays, where fishing, snorkeling, and diving are the main attractions. There are over 600 Mayan sites to explore, while the many national parks, protected reserves, and special development areas are an integral part of the eco-tourism program. Eco-tourism combines tourism with environmental and natural history interests.

Tourism was initially slow to get off the ground in the 1960s when other countries were developing as tourist destinations. At that time, tourism did not have the whole-hearted support of the ruling British government. There was some feeling that as the country was nearing self-government and independence, and was about to cut its ties to Great Britain, that it did not need more foreigners entering Belize. However, by the 1980s, a tourist boom was in full swing, and in the 1990s only sugar brought more foreign exchange into the country.

Some people are now concerned at the impact tourism is having on Belize. Most of the best hotels and lodges are owned by foreigners, and in San Pedro on Ambergris Cay, where it all started, most of the tourist industry is controlled by United States investors. Although the local population is now better off, land prices have soared, and half the population of the island is now foreign. Locals say the marine environment is being damaged. Some other cays are still virtually uninhabited and relatively untouched by tourism, and a few have become the base of conservation programs studying the reef.

It was announced in 1991 that Belize was to become the center of Mundo Maya, a joint project among Mexico, Belize, Guatemala, Honduras, and El Salvador. The idea originated when the American National Geographic Society saw a way to link major Mayan sites in the five countries by one tourist circuit. Visitors can see ancient Maya sites and living Maya cultures with more organized travel schedules and easier border crossings. The project has received financial help from the European Community.

DRUGS

It is difficult to assess the value of the illegal drugs trade on the Belizean economy. Some people believe it to be the country's top business. A few years ago the trade was in marijuana. Small farmers found it much more profitable than growing corn and beans, and at one time Belize was the fourth largest supplier of marijuana to the United States. In an attempt to kill the business, the United States supplied the Belizean police with airplanes and chemicals for a spraying campaign designed to eliminate the crop. It was largely successful, though some marijuana is still grown.

Marijuana has been replaced by the cocaine business. Cocaine is not produced in Belize, but the country has become part of the route the drug travels from South American countries to the United States. Because it is illegal, there is no certain way of knowing how much money it brings into the country, but wealth and "drug money" are obvious in some border towns. Many people, from all levels of society, including the police and government, benefit from the business, making it very difficult to stop.

TRADING WITH THE WORLD

Belize trades mainly with the United States, the European Community, United Kingdom (Britain), Mexico, and Jamaica. In a typical year—1993—it exported to the United States almost 40 percent of its goods, to the European Community 32 percent, and to the United Kingdom 29.5 percent. Imports from the same countries amounted to more than 50 percent from the United States, about 21 percent from the European Community, and 12.6 percent from Britain. While agricultural products and clothing make up most of the exports, imports range from machinery and transport equipment, electronic goods, food, such as wheat, Dutch condensed milk, and some canned meats, together with all the petroleum the country needs.

Belize regularly imports more than it exports, and the trade

Belize exports in small quantities chicle, collected from the sap of the sapodilla tree (left), for use in chewing gum, and fabrics typical of the Central American Indians (above).

deficit representing the difference between income and expenditure is gradually increasing. This is partly because the government is investing in new projects, such as hydroelectricity, transport, and hotels. Belize needs a good trade surplus if it is to pay off its international debt and be less reliant on financial support from the United States. Its international debt, which is money borrowed from foreign governments and banks, is not as large as that of many developing countries, but it is increasing. Financial aid and investment from the United States are evident in many of the important industries in Belize, including the new boom in hotel building and in agriculture, oil exploration, and garment factories. At the same time, Belize's trade deficit with the United States has steadily worsened. From 1980 to 1990, it grew by over $21 million.

Very important to the Belize economy is the preferential quota arrangements it has with the United States and the European Community. Belize has been able to sell about a fifth of its sugar to the United States at prices higher than those of the world market. And the Caribbean Basin Initiative, instigated by the United States government in 1984, allows Belize and other countries to sell, among other foodstuffs, fruit to the United States free of import tax. The arrangement with the European Community comes under the Lomé Convention, which benefits some sixty developing countries. Certain foodstuffs sold by these countries to the Community carry very little tax, and sales are guaranteed. Belize is also a member of CARICOM, the Caribbean Community and Common Market. As the largest producer of citrus fruit in the area, it can presently sell without fear of competition from countries outside the Caribbean.

But plans are already in hand to introduce more free trade, with everyone trading on the same terms and without tax benefits. In 1993 Canada, Mexico, and the United States signed the North American Free Trade Agreement (NAFTA), creating the largest free trade block in the world. The Lomé Convention may change as a result of the expansion of the European Community, and there is a fear, too, that CARICOM may opt for free trade. If all this were to happen, Belize's small economy, reliant on just a few commodities, would be severely hit.

ROLE IN THE WORLD

In defining its role in the world, Belize has first to come to terms with its own identity. Although Belizeans considered themselves first and foremost Belizeans, the fact remains that the population is made up of different peoples from a variety of backgrounds. As a result of its long association with Britain, with

The American Embassy is still located in Belize City. The United States plays an important role in the economic development of Belize.

English as the official language, and many aspects of life, such as the legal system, government, and education based on the British system, Belize might well consider itself to have more in common with the West Indian islands than with the countries of Central America. Most Creoles have their roots in Africa or the West Indies. Yet, as more Spanish speakers arrive, and with the mestizo population now the largest group in the country, Belize has to question where its future lies. For the moment, with the Guatemala dispute seemingly resolved, Belize seems to be content to be part of both worlds.

An added complication is its relationship with the United States. For many years now, the United States has had a stronger presence in Belize than Britain. Belize is heavily dependent on the United States for financial, economic, and social aid, and North American culture has more influence than any other. For its part, the United States recognizes Belize as a neutral and politically stable country in a region which, particularly during the 1980s, experienced civil wars, dictatorships, and terrorist activity. The 1990s has brought a degree of peace to most of Central America, but the United States is always mindful that it might need a military base in the area, and Belize would be the obvious choice.

FUTURE

As with many developing countries, Belize, of course, has problems. The population is still small, though there is not the extreme poverty that exists in other parts of Latin America. The roads and energy sources needed to run a successful economy were almost completely ignored while Belize was a colony, but improvements are now being made to the transport system.

The economy is still reliant on too few commodities and subject to variations in the market, which are beyond Belize's control. With such a small industrial base, imports into Belize remain too high. The discovery of oil or gas or the further development of hydroelectrical energy could help ease the problem. But in the short term, Belize is hoping that tourism will boost the economy. The prospects are bright, particularly as the emphasis is on eco-tourism, and consideration is already being given to ensuring that the environment is not damaged by a great influx of tourists. Belize has an immense wealth in the flora and fauna of the barrier reef, its coast, and its forests, and these must be safeguarded for the benefit of future generations of Belizeans.

In the few years since Belize gained independence, it has emerged from being, as some would say, a backwater colony into a stable, democratic country. Several elections have been held and power passed between the two main political parties, peacefully and without discord. Much of the success of its stability derives from its history and is based on the relationship built up between the various peoples who settled in the country. Together they fought for self-government, and today they are working together for a better future.

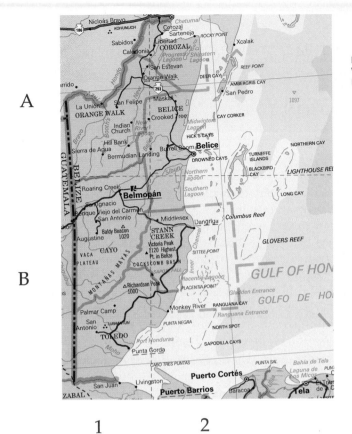

A

B

1   2

Map from Cosmopolitan Series Mexico
Wall Map © 1995 by Rand McNally,
R.L. 95-S-245

MINI-FACTS AT A GLANCE

GENERAL INFORMATION

Official Name: Belize

Capital: Belmopan

Government: Belize is a parliamentary democracy and a constitutional monarchy with Queen Elizabeth II as head of state. The National Assembly has two houses, the Senate with 8 appointed members and the House of Representatives with 29 elected members. The British Monarch is represented by a governor general who must be a Belizean citizen. The prime minister is the leader of the majority party in the House and is the head of government. Both the prime minister and the cabinet members come from the majority party in the National Assembly. The legal system is based on English law. The highest court of justice is the Supreme Court. For administrative purposes, the country is divided into six districts: Belize, Cayo, Corozal, Orange Walk, Stann Creek, and Toledo.

Religion: Belize is a secular country where constitution does not support any state religion. The majority of the Belizeans are Roman Catholics. Other groups include the Anglicans, the Methodists, and some evangelical sects such as the Assemblies of God, Baptists, Seventh Day Adventists, Jehovah's Witnesses, and the Mormons. Mennonites are northern European immigrants who have settled in Belize. They follow a strict religious and moral code. The Baha'i faith is followed by some 3 percent of the population.

Ethnic Composition: The mestizos, the Creoles, the Maya, and the Garifuna (Black Caribs) largely make up the Belizean population. The 1991 census shows that mestizos make up about 44 percent of the population, Creoles 30 percent, Mayas 11 percent, Garifunas 7 percent, and the rest are immigrants. Mestizos are descendants of marriages between the Native Indians and Europeans; Creoles are descended from marriages between African slaves and the Europeans; Garifunas are descended from marriages between African slaves and Carib Indians of the West Indies. Most of these groups dominate a particular region of the country. The population of Belize City is more than 50 percent Creole. Indians, Chinese, Lebanese, Syrians, and north Europeans (Mennonites) are the major immigrant groups.

Language: English is the official language. The English used by Creoles is a patois of English mixed with local Creole words and foreign expressions; it is spoken with a sing-song lilt. Spanish is the language of the mestizos. There is also a form of Creole Spanish. The Mennonites speak a German-Dutch dialect, and different dialects of the Mayan language are spoken by the Maya Indians.

National Flag: The flag consists of a wide dark-blue stripe with narrow horizontal red stripes at the upper and lower edges. At the center is a large white disk bearing the state coat of arms bordered by a wreath of green leaves.

National Emblem: The shield of the coat of arms is divided into three sections by an inverted letter V. The base depicts a ship in full sail; the two upper portions show the tools of the timber industry. Supporting the shield are two woodcutters. A mahogany tree rises above the shield at the top. Beneath the shield is a scroll with the motto *Sub Umbra Floreo* (Under the Shade I Flourish).

National Anthem: "O the Land of the Free by the Carib Sea"

National Calendar: Gregorian

Money: Belizean dollar (BZ$) is a paper currency of 100 cents; it has the same fractional coins as the U.S. dollar. In December 1995 one Belizean dollar was worth $0.50 in United States currency.

Membership in International Organizations: Caribbean Community and Common Market (CARICOM), Caribbean Development Bank (CDB); Commonwealth of Nations; Group of 77 (G-77); Inter-American Development Bank (IDB); International Monetary Fund (IMF); Nonaligned Movement (NAM); Organization of American States (OAS); United Nations (UN)

Weights and Measures: Metric system except for gasoline, which is measured in U.S. gallons.

Population: 1994 estimates 210,000; density 23 persons per sq. mi. (9 persons per sq km), of which 46 percent live in towns and 54 percent in rural areas. It is one of the most sparsely populated countries in the Central America.

Cities: Belize City 47,700
            Orange Walk 11,9
            San Ignacio/Santa Elena 9,700
            Corozal 7,600
            Dangriga 7,000
            Belmopan 3,900
    (Population based on 1993 estimates)

GEOGRAPHY

Border: Mexico is to the north and northwest, and Guatemala is to the south and west. The Caribbean Sea makes the eastern border. Belize is the second smallest country in Central America after El Salvador.

Coastline: Caribbean coastline is 174 mi. (280 km) long. Belize is the only country in Central America without a coastline on the North Pacific Ocean.

Land: The northern part is a swampy lowland less than 200 ft. (60 m) above sea level; these lowlands are interrupted only by the Manatee Hills. The southern half is dominated by the Maya Mountains that run parallel to the coast. A narrow coastal plain separates the coast from the mountains. The coastline is heavily indented with many lagoons that are filled with mangrove vegetation. A group of small coral islands, called the Cays, are offshore in the Caribbean Sea. The Turneffe Islands, a group of small atolls, are nearby. A barrier reef teeming with marine life extends for 150 mi. (240 km) just offshore. It is the longest of its kind in the western hemisphere. The United Nations Environment Program has declared this barrier reef to be unique on account of its untouched condition with the sponges, corals, and fish.

Highest Point: Victoria Peak (3,680 ft. [1,122 m]).

Lowest Point: Along the Caribbean Sea coast.

Rivers: The Hondo River marks the boundary with Mexico in the north. The New River in the northwest has long been used for transporting timber and logs. The Macal River, rising in the Maya Mountains, and the Belize River, rising in the Petén region of Guatemala, drain to the Caribbean Sea in the south. Belizean rivers are largely bordered by swamp vegetation. There are numerous small rivers with short courses. Sarstoon River forms Belize's southern boundary.

Forests: Some 45 percent of land is forested with at least 50 different tree species. Northern forests are generally broad leaved and deciduous; date palm, mahogany, and ironwood predominate. Palm forests grow on the clay soils while mixed pine and oak forests are on the sandy soils. Maya Mountains are covered with a cloud forest—a leafy wilderness of ferns, bromeliads, and masses of orchids. Forests are Belize's most important natural resource providing logwood, mahogany, medicinal plants, orchids, chicle (for making chewing gum), rubber, natural oil, and nuts. Some two-thirds of the wood cut annually is used for fuel. Government has introduced reforestation with some fast-growing trees. Some 90 percent of Belize's coastal mangrove forests are preserved in their natural state.

Guanacaste Park, Crooked Tree Wildlife Sanctuary, Community Baboon Sanctuary, Mountain Pine Ridge, and Blue Hole National Park are some of Belize's wildlife and nature reserves. Belize also has a jaguar reserve—the first of its kind in the world.

Wildlife: A small cowlike animal, the tapir, is the country's national animal. Wildlife includes jaguar, wild pig, puma (cougar), margay, coatimundi, kinkajous, and ocelot. The black howler monkeys, also called baboons, are now rare. The manatee or sea cow lives in the warm waters of rivers and bays. A variety of snakes like pit viper and coral snakes abound. Iguanas (lizards) can reach up to 3 ft. (1 m) in length and are often eaten in the countryside. The American crocodile and three sea turtles—hawkbill, green, and leatherback—are on the endangered animals list.

Belize has a varied birdlife ranging from tiny hummingbirds to brilliant macaws and toucans with massive bills. The jabiru stork is one of the largest flying birds in the Americas. Waterbirds include the boat-billed herons, snake bird (anhinga), ducks, egrets, kingfisher, white ibis, and frigatebird.

Climate: The climate is subtropical with a distinct wet season that lasts from June to October and a dry season from February to April. The seasons are marked by the difference in humidity; the average humidity at 83 percent is very high. Climate is moderated by the Caribbean trade winds which keep annual temperatures between 60° F to 90° F (15° C to 32° C) in the coastal region and slightly higher inland. Rainfall is more abundant in the south, sometimes averaging 180 in. (458 cm) but the northern parts are drier. Rain falls almost every day, except during the dry season (February to May). Hurricanes are a constant threat in the hurricane season, which lasts from September to November.

Greatest Distance: North-South, 174 mi. (280 km)
East-West 70 mi. (112 km)
Area: 8,866 sq. mi. (22,962 sq km)

ECONOMY AND INDUSTRY

Agriculture: Less than 5 percent of the land is actually under agriculture, but about half of the working population is employed in agriculture. Major cash crops are sugarcane, citrus fruits, papayas, mangoes, vegetables, cocoa, and bananas. Rice, corn, sweet potatoes, yams, and kidney beans are the principal domestic crops. Some coconuts and soybeans are also grown. Sugar exports account for one-third of the total export income. Cattle and pigs are raised to supplement farm income. Mennonites are engaged in commercial farming and have started a dairy industry. Honey is produced on commercial farms.

Fish are plentiful in the Belizean waters and fishing is mainly done by cooperatives. Catfish, barracuda, tarpon, butterfly fish, grunts, and groupers are common. Lobster, sea turtle, and conch are very popular. Much of the fish is frozen or canned for export. There is a danger of overfishing in the Belizean waters.

Mining: Belize does not have energy resources, and most of the petroleum is imported. Some petroleum was discovered in the northern part in 1981, but it is not being produced in commercial quantities. Energy supply is supplemented with locally produced hydroelectricity. There are very few mineral resources such as limestone, sand, and gravel.

Manufacturing: Manufacturing employs some 15 percent of the total work force. It includes clothing, sugar refining, and food processing (beer and soft drinks), cigarettes, fertilizer, animal feed, furniture, and building materials.

Molasses is made from sugarcane and is used in the production of ethanol. Local rum is also made from sugar. Citrus fruits are turned into concentrate for export.

Tourism: Tourism is becoming very important for the Belizean economy. The majority of the tourists are from the United States. The main tourist attraction is the barrier reef and the cays, with fishing, snorkeling, and diving facilities. The ruins of Mayan ceremonial sites, particularly of Caracol and Xunantunich, attract many tourists; there are some 600 Maya sites to explore. Belize's eco-tourism combines tourism with environmental and natural history interests.

Transportation: There are no railroads in the country. In the early 1990s there were 1,287 mi. (2,070 km) of roads, of which some 20 percent were paved. The Northern Highway, the Western Highway, and the Hummingbird Highway are the major roads. Belize does not have a national airline but is served by several international airlines. There are eight airports, with the international airport at Belize City. Maya Airways flies daily locally. A deepwater port is at Belize City and a second port is at Commerce Bight, near Dangriga. The Big Creek port handles mainly bananas and citrus fruits. Inland navigable waterways have been in use to transport logs and timber to the coastal ports for a long time. Regular ferry and boat services carry passengers around the cays.

Communication: Belize has no daily newspaper, but there are six weekly publications. Most of the newspapers are in English. Radio broadcasts are in both English and Spanish. Television is relatively new. The press is free from censorship, and television and radio are not under government control either. The telephone service is good and efficient. In the early 1990s, there was one radio receiver per 2 persons, one television set per 8 persons, and one telephone per 8 persons.

Trade: Chief imports are machinery and transport equipment, food items, consumer goods, and fuels. Major import sources are United States, Mexico, United Kingdom, Netherlands, and Guatemala. Chief export items are sugar, oranges and orange concentrate, clothes, bananas, and grapefruits. Major export destinations are United States, United Kingdom, Mexico, Canada, and Germany.

EVERYDAY LIFE

Health: Belize enjoys a better health and welfare system than other Central American countries. Medical care is mostly free. Major diseases are cancer and pneumonia. Yellow fever and smallpox have been eradicated, but malaria is still a threat. The majority of the hospitals, dental clinics, and child-care facilities are run by the state. Countryside is served by rural and mobile clinics. Some 60 percent of the population has access to safe drinking water.

Life expectancy at 67 years for males and 72 years for females is high. Infant mortality rate at 37 per 1,000 is high.

Education: Education is compulsory for all children for eight years between the ages of 5 and 14 years. Primary education lasts for eight years and is provided free of charge. The majority of the primary schools are run by the Roman Catholic Church. Schools are funded jointly by the government and their respective church organizations. Secondary education lasts for four or five years. St. John's College is a prestigious Jesuit secondary school in Belize City. Other educational institutes include technical, vocational, and teacher-training colleges. Higher education is provided by the University College of Belize and a branch of the University of West Indies in Belize. The country's best-educated people tend to migrate to other English-speaking countries in search of better futures. In the early 1990s, the literacy rate was about 94 percent, one of the highest in the Latin America.

Holidays: January 1, New Year's Day
March 9, Baron Bliss Day
April 5-8, Easter
May 1, Labour Day
May 24, Commonwealth Day
September 10, St. George's Cay Day
September 21, National Independence Day
October 12, Columbus Day
November 19, Garifuna Settlement Day
December 25, Christmas

Culture: Belizean culture is largely associated with the English-speaking Caribbean countries and Great Britain. The country is noted for its cultural diversity, which ranges from European to African-oriented Creole culture to the Mayan and indigenous elements. Social and racial conflicts are almost non-existent. Mayan civilization artifacts are exhibited in the Baron Bliss Institute in Belize City and at the Department of Archaeology at Belmopan. Belize City also is home of the Institute for Arts and Drama and the National Library. The remains of the ancient Maya civilization are being excavated by the government with international help.

Society: Extended families are common. Grandparents often take care of children. Single mothers are not unusual among Creoles. Formal marriages are becoming less important as many women remain unmarried even after having children.

Dress: People in urban areas wear Western-style clothing. At public places such as banks, hotels, and offices, workers wear uniforms. In rural areas, Maya women sometimes still wear traditional bright-colored long skirts with white blouses. Garifuna women wear head scarves and colorful blouses and skirts.

Housing: The majority of houses are built of wood, with corrugated iron roofs, and several windows. Many homes are built on wooden or concrete stilts to avoid possible floods. The lower rooms are used only for kitchen or storage. An average home may have two to three rooms, shared by possibly two or three generations of one family. Most homes have sanitation facilities and electricity. In rural areas, wooden houses have roofing of coconut thatch. Some homes are built of flattened metal strips. Rural mestizos live in adobe brick houses. A variety of colorful tropical trees and plants surround the rural houses. In cities there is a shortage of housing; the government has built several low-cost projects to ease the shortage. Belize's housing situation is aggravated by periodic hurricane devastations.

Food: Traditional food is a mix of Creole, Mexican, Chinese, and European dishes. Chicken with rice, beans, or plantains is the national dish. White rice and kidney beans are common throughout Belize. Mangoes, bananas, and oranges are part of the staple diet. Maize and beans are staple food for the Maya. Tortillas made from maize are filled with chicken, meat, or cheese and are covered in a spicy sauce. The Maya hunt iguana, duck, pig, agouti, and gibnuts for food. Local fresh fish is an important aspect of Belizean food. Lobster, conch, shrimp, red snapper, sea bass, halibut, and barracuda are cooked in many ways. A "boil-up" is a seafood stew seasoned with onions and peppers. Seafood gumbo is made of conch, lobster, shrimp, coconut milk, plantains, and herbs and served with rice.

Sports and Recreation: Soccer is very popular as is basketball, but organized sports are limited to some private clubs only. Women play softball. The cross-country cycle race around Easter time is internationally renowned. Water sports such as scuba diving, swimming, snorkeling, boating, and fishing are very popular.

Music and dance in Belize are influenced by the rhythms and beats of Africa, the Caribbean, and modern pop music from Europe and the United States. Creole folk songs are melodious. The "break-down" songs have their origin in the logging camps and are accompanied by steel bands, banjos, guitars, and harmonicas. The marimba (a wooden xylophone), violins, harps, and guitars are the most popular musical instruments. Belizeans enjoy reggae, calypso, and Caribbean rock called punta rock based on Garifuna music. The ethnic Maya dances are the Tiger Dance and the Holy Deer Dance. The country's most important indigenous festival is Dangriga's Settlement Day, with Caribbean songs and dances. Carnival celebrates St. George's Cay Day with a street party and parade. Christmas is celebrated as a family-oriented religious holiday.

Social Welfare: Social welfare laws were first enacted in 1979. These include old-age, invalidity, death insurance, and sickness and maternity insurance. Social security benefits are provided to sick, disabled, and unemployed workers. Families tend to take care of older and sick relatives at home.

IMPORTANT DATES

A.D. 900—Probable time of the collapse of Maya civilization

1502—Christopher Columbus sees Belize on his fourth voyage to the Americas.

1603—Peter Wallace, a Scottish pirate, sets up a camp in Belize.

1638—Shipwrecked English sailors start a settlement that will later become Belize City.

1670—A treaty between Spain and Britain gives Baymen permission to continue cutting logwood.

1675—A ship carrying West African slaves is shipwrecked near Belize.

1713—Treaty of Utrecht forces Spaniards to give up their monopoly on carrying goods to and from Spanish America.

1718—A group of Spanish and Indian soldiers arrive in Belize.

1720—Black slaves from Africa start arriving in the Bay settlement area.

1733—Spaniards demolish the town of Belize.

1739—Belize is attacked again as the result of war between England and Spain.

1754—Loggers win a notable victory by defeating Spanish forces.

1763—By signing the Treaty of Paris, British agree to destroy the fort at Belize City.

1764—British appoint an official to plan a system of self-government for the Bay Settlement.

1783—By the Treaty of Versailles Spain grants settlers some concessions.

1784—British government appoints its first Superintendent to oversee the affairs of the settlement.

1796—War breaks out between Spain and England.

1798—Spain is finally defeated, and Belize comes under control of England.

1802—Garifuna's traditional date of arrival in Belize.

1812—St. John's Cathedral is built; it is the oldest Anglican church in Central America.

1814—The Government House is built in Belize City.

1816—The first school is opened in Belize by the Church of England.

1823—Slavery is abolished in Central America.

1826—Britain makes a treaty with Mexico that allows Belize to continue much as before.

1838—Slavery is finally abolished in Belize.

1857—Some 1,000 Indian soldiers are brought by the British to Belize to work on the sugar plantations.

1859—Guatemala and England agree to try and resolve their claims over Belize; the Belize Estate and Produce Company owns one-fifth of the entire country.

1862—England agrees to make Belize a British Crown Colony.

1871—Belize becomes British Honduras, a British Crown Colony.

1913—First citrus fruit, grapefruit, is planted.

1919—Race riots break out between the Creoles and British.

1931—Death toll reaches 2,500 in one day from a hurricane, and the banana crop is devastated.

1945—In a new constitution, Guatemala refers to Belize as the 23rd department of that country.

1949—British Honduran dollar is devalued.

1950—People's United Party (PUP) wins the City Council elections.

1954—Because of voter discrimination, there are only 822 registered voters in the colony; a new constitution gives all Belize adults the right to vote.

1955—Hurricane Janet devastates Corozal.

1959—Some 3,000 Mennonites arrive in Belize.

1960—Legislative Assembly reforms take place.

1961—Hurricane Hattie causes severe devastation in Belize.

1964—A National Assembly is created with a House of Representatives and a Senate.

1965—It is agreed by both Belize and Guatemala that a U.S. attorney should be appointed as a mediator; site is cleared in a dry forest area for the new capital city of Belmopan.

1970—Capital is moved from Belize City to Belmopan.

1973—British Honduras officially adopts the name *Belize.*

1975—Toledo Maya Cultural Council is established to protect Maya culture and defend their rights.

1976—Talks begin once more for Belize's independence.

1978—Hurricane Greta brings torrential rains for two straight weeks; Belize Defence Force is formed from the existing Police Force and a Volunteer Guard.

1980—Belize wins an important resolution in the United Nations that almost guarantees its independence.

1981—Belize gains independence; George Price of PUP becomes prime minister; Guatemala refuses to recognize Belize's independence and presses territorial claims.

1984—Elections are held; Manuel Esquivel of United Democratic Party (UDM) is elected prime minister; the U.S. removes taxes from the citrus fruits grown in the Caribbean, thus boosting citrus crop in Belize.

1985—The Belize Sugar Industries becomes the largest sugar industry in the country.

1986—University College of Belize is established.

1987—A Guatemalan trade delegation visits Belize—the first since Belize became independent.

1988—A joint commission is established to examine territorial dispute with Guatemala.

1989—PUP wins again in general election, Price becomes prime minister.

1990—Belize holds official talks with Guatemala in an effort to settle the border dispute.

1991—Belize becomes a member of the Organization of American States; Prime Minister George Price reaches an agreement with President Jorge Serrano of Guatemala; Belize is to become the center of the Mundo Maya joint project between Mexico, Belize, Guatemala, Honduras, and El Salvador.

1992—Belize becomes a member of International Development Bank (IDB).

1993—George Price loses the elections; four ancient Maya villages dating back to A.D. 700 are discovered.

1994—Some 1,500 British troops withdraw from Belize; a 6,000-acre (2,428-hectare) rain-forest sanctuary is created to protect medicinal plants in the Terra Nova Forest Reserve.

1995—A summit meeting of CARICOM leaders is held in Belize.

IMPORTANT PEOPLE

Baron Bliss, also known as Henry Edward Ernest Bliss, a Portuguese Baron born in England; he put two million dollars in trust to benefit Belize in return for the kindness he received from the Belizean people in 1926 when he was sick; many public works have been financed by the interest of this money; Belizeans pay tribute to him on March 9th, Baron Bliss Day.

Manuel Esquivel (1940–), leader of the UDP; became prime minister in 1984, and again in 1993

Philip Goldson, a leader of People's United Party (PUP)

George Cadle Price (1919–), leader of the PUP; became country's first prime minister in 1964 and was elected again in 1989

Colville Young, governor general in the early 1990s

Nelson Young, contemporary Belizean artist

Compiled by Chandrika Kaul, Ph.D.

INDEX

Page numbers that appear in boldface type indicate illustrations

About the Author

Newly graduated with a degree in history from the University of Wales, Marion Morrison first traveled to South America in 1962 with a British volunteer program to work among Aymara Indians living near Lake Titicaca. In Bolivia she met her husband, British filmmaker and writer Tony Morrison. During the last thirty years, the Morrisons, who make their home in England, have visited almost every country in South and Central America, making television documentary films, photographing, and researching—often accompanied by their children, Kimball and Rebecca.

Marion Morrison has written about South and Central American countries for many publishers, including six other books in the Enchantment of the World series. From their travels, the Morrisons have created their South American Picture Library, which contains more than one hundred thousand images of the continent.